CHOMP!

Fierce facts about the *BITE FORCE*, *CRUSHING JAWS*, and *MIGHTY TEETH* of Earth's champion chewers

NATIONAL GEOGRAPHIC

WASHINGTON, D.C.

BRADY BARR

Extreme Animal Explorer

Contents

I'M LUCKY TO HAVE WHAT I THINK IS ONE OF THE WORLD'S COOLEST JOBS. I am a ***HERPETOLOGIST,*** a scientist who works with reptiles and amphibians. I'm an expert on crocodiles. They're my specialty and my passion. In my work as an animal expert for National Geographic, I travel the world to interact with some of the most ***AMAZING ANIMALS*** on the planet.

Every job, though, has its challenges. For me, it's the ***BITING.***

Often, in order to learn more about fascinating creatures, I must get up close—really close—into the ***BITE ZONE.*** Bites can and do happen. For me, taking a bite every so often was worth it, because I wanted to learn more about animals to better help ***PROTECT THEM.*** But that didn't mean I wanted to always be a chew toy!

I decided I'd better start doing my bite homework. I needed to research animals' ***BITING ABILITIES*** to decrease my chances of getting hurt. I learned as much as I could about the animals before I encountered them in the wild. I studied what ***KIND OF TEETH*** they have, ***WHAT THEY EAT,*** and ***WHERE THEY LIVE.*** I wanted to know ***HOW THEY USE THEIR BITES.*** Are the bites venomous? Fast? Strong? How do an animal's skull and muscles power its bites?

The more I learned, the more I wanted to know.

By looking at why and how one animal bites, I could relate what I learned to other animals. For example, ***BITING ISN'T JUST FOR FEEDING.*** Animals can use their bites for defense, courtship, maintaining territories, and challenging rivals. By looking at

animal skulls and skeletons, I better understood how animals live and survive by their bites—not just today, but also for extinct animals that lived long ago. But most importantly, I learned how to more safely interact with these creatures without getting bitten!

One thing I definitely had to keep in mind was an animal's ***BITE FORCE.*** That's how much pressure the animal applies when it bites down. I was surprised that the bite force of many animals was unknown. No one had ever measured them before—or had been crazy enough to try! I asked the engineers at National Geographic to build me a ***DYNAMOMETER.*** (That's a fancy word for bite-force meter.) On every expedition, I took along my trusty dynamometer and measured the bite force of animals I encountered.

Most of the bite-force numbers you read in this book are from my own measurements. There's more than one way to measure bites, but I always measure bites in pounds of force. That's what you will see throughout this book. I've also organized these animals into four different groups, based on how I perceive them to chomp!

I guarantee that, after you read this book, ***YOU'LL NEVER LOOK AT A TOOTHY ANIMAL GRIN IN THE SAME WAY.*** I hope you enjoy reading this book as much as I enjoyed writing it. Remember: A lot of bites went into making it!

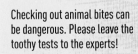

Checking out animal bites can be dangerous. Please leave the toothy tests to the experts!

CHAPTER 1

GRIPPERS

Holding on tight is what this group of animals does best, thanks to their LOCK-DOWN GRIPPING BITE. If any of these chompers get a hold of you, you're not going anywhere anytime soon!

Lights, Camera, Action ...
(Not That Action!!!)

THE BLISTERING MIDDAY HEAT brought everything to a standstill on the African savanna. Our National Geographic film crew had been following a pride of lions for days, waiting and sweating in the sweltering sun to record daytime feeding—but the lions only napped instead!

We devised a plan. We would sacrifice our steak dinner that evening to draw in the pride for filming. That steak looked tasty, and I was super hungry, but we needed this footage.

We drove a distance in front of the pride and tied our bait to a tree. We placed four small video cameras around the steak to get close-up footage of the lions feeding. I put three of the cameras on the ground near the bait and one up in the tree pointing down.

My producer asked, "Brady, shouldn't we hide the cameras so the lions can't see them?" I laughed and said, "No need. Those hungry lions will be so focused on the meat that they won't even look at our cameras!"

The lions were coming, so we sped off to wait at a safe distance. They trotted in, excited by the smell of the bait. They quickly circled the meat. Our crew was thrilled at the thought of the feeding footage we were about to get. All of a sudden, one lion rushed straight past the bait and grabbed one of the cameras in its jaws. Then a second lion grabbed a camera, and two other lions began fighting over the third camera! The lions were ignoring our meat and crushing our cameras instead! I couldn't believe what was happening! "This is really bad," I thought. Suddenly, all the lions ran off with our cameras in their mouths. I was dumbfounded. My mouth hung open.

I thought to myself, "At least we have the camera in the tree." But, out of the blue, one lion ran back and jumped into the tree. It snatched our last camera in its jaws and then dashed off into the bush. The crew stood in shocked silence. **Who knew that lions had a taste for TV cameras?**

AFRICAN LION

MEET THE BEAST

THERE'S A REASON THE LION IS CALLED THE KING OF BEASTS! Our first gripper is a heavyweight that tips the scales at almost **500 pounds** (227 kg), stands over three feet (0.9 m) tall, and is nearly eight feet (2.4 m) long. Lions have muscular front legs and strong shoulders, along with sharp retractable claws and massive teeth that, combined, make them well-armed hunters. Their oversize canines are one of the first things you notice about this cat ... but hopefully not the last!

DID YOU KNOW?

IF A LION LICKED YOUR FACE with its raspy tongue, your cheek would be bloodied after a few seconds. Note to self: Avoid lion kisses.

BITE FORCE

A LION'S BITE FORCE HAS BEEN MEASURED at around 700 pounds (318 kg), and it could be more. Lions want to avoid breaking their teeth, especially on a hard bite-force meter! So it's been hard to get a good reading.

1²3 BY THE NUMBERS

A LION HAS THE SAME NUMBER OF TEETH as your house cat (30), but its canines are an impressive three inches (7.6 cm) long!

BITE BUSINESS

Just like your house cat, lions have claws, too. A lion attack starts when the lion flexes muscles to shoot out those daggerlike claws. Once the lion digs its powerful claws deep in its prey, its strong upper body, arms, and jaws come into play. The lion holds on tightly to bring down the struggling animal. Often prey is killed quickly with a **strong bite** to the back of the neck. The lion's large canines are spaced far enough apart to fall in between the neck vertebrae of prey. They cut the spinal cord and cause instant death. At other times, a powerful bite to the nose or neck suffocates prey.

A lion's teeth make quick work of a meal, so they can eat their fill before hyenas arrive. The meat-cutting carnassial back teeth work like scissors to shear off meat chunks. They are set into a very rigid jawbone that doesn't move side to side like your jaw does. **This holds the food steadier,** so it's easier to cut through. If that doesn't sound deadly enough, a lion's tongue even has recurved teeth, or spines, called papillae, that are used to scrape skin from meat and meat from bone!

WHAT'S ON THE
MENU

LIONS are obligate carnivores. That means animals from A (antelope) to Z (zebra) and all grassland animals in between are on the menu. When you have a hungry pride to feed, big spreads are always good, so giant prey is a bonus. **Giraffes, rhinos, and hippos** are all on the dinner plate for a hungry pride of lions. Big animals are not easy to bring down, so it takes a group effort to tackle those jumbos. When the group is successful, there are second helpings for everyone. I'll have more hippopotamus, please!

GIRAFFE

TASMANIAN DEVIL

MEET THE BEAST

THE TASMANIAN DEVIL IS NOT REALLY LIKE the spitting, mumbling, whirling tornado-like cartoon character. However, it is pretty goofy looking. It looks front-heavy, with a big chunky head and powerful shoulders and neck. Its front legs are longer than its back legs, making its hind end look underfed! Watch out for the front end, though; it can be one tough customer. The devil gets its name from its habit of screaming and sounding ferocious!

DID YOU KNOW?

THE SCIENTIFIC NAME of the Tasmanian devil means "meat lover." However, it's probably not a good idea to invite this guy to your backyard barbecue!

123 BY THE NUMBERS

DEVILS HAVE 42 NONREPLACEABLE TEETH that grow continuously. The molars are bone crushers. The oversize canines are about an inch (2.5 cm) long.

MENU

When you're a **SCREAMING DEVIL,** you eat anything and everything you want! Their bone-cracking teeth make them excellent scavengers; no leftovers are too tough for them. But when devils must actually hunt for food, their canines are up to the task. They surprise unsuspecting victims, chase them down over short distances, and then kill with a powerful bite. Devils have been known to go after **fish, reptiles, moths, birds, platypuses, wallabies,** and just about anything else they can catch. Devils seem to have a special fondness for nice fat wombats. (Who wouldn't?)

BITE BUSINESS

At a feeding, devils are like noisy, rude, out-of-control dinner guests. When a devil finds a carcass and begins to eat, it gets excited and starts **screaming and growling.** That attracts other devils; it's like ringing the dinner bell! Before long, there is a mob of devils. They push, jostle, snap, and quickly wolf down as much meat as they can. They can eat 40 percent of their body weight in a single feeding. Their jaws open extra wide, to around 80 degrees (about the same range as a *T. rex*). This allows them to bolt down extra-big pieces of meat. After dinner, there's not much left of the carcass because the devils' teeth are designed as bone crackers.

Tasmanian devils are **good hunters.** If a devil didn't get an invitation to the carcass dinner party, no worries! It surprises prey, sometimes much larger than itself, and brings it down with a massive crushing bite to the skull or neck. Those honking big canines are great for skull penetration. Plus, a devil's oversize head (one-third of its body weight) is chock-full of powerful muscles that are the driving force behind those killer canines and bone-cracking molars.

BITE FORCE

WITH A BITE FORCE OF AROUND 400 POUNDS (181 KG), it's got a lot of bite for such a small 20-pound (9-kg) animal. Tasmanian devils can bite through metal wire!

GRAY WOLF

MEET THE BEAST

DON'T BE FOOLED: The gray wolf is gray only in name. Its colors can be gray, tan, brown, black, and even white. This slender apex predator is the largest wild member of the dog family. It stands almost three feet (0.9 m) tall, measures six feet (1.8 m) long from nose to tail, and weighs up to 150 pounds (68 kg). A gray wolf's strong neck, large head, and long muzzle are all signs of a powerful bite!

WHAT'S ON THE
MENU

With so many mouths to feed, **WOLF PACKS** tend to go after large prey. Big ungulates (animals with hooves) like **deer, moose, bison, and elk** are all on the menu. The pack usually targets sick, old, or injured prey that would be easier to chase and take down. When they don't have the power of the pack, single wolves go after smaller prey like **rabbits, mice, voles, and even insects like grasshoppers.** Sometimes wolves will even eat berries or scavenge a rotting carcass. Wolves can go weeks without food if they have to. (But who wants to?)

DID YOU KNOW?

WOLVES FEED THEIR YOUNG by vomiting up food from their stomachs. Would you like to see your mom do that at the breakfast table?

BITE FORCE

A GRAY WOLF'S BITE FORCE IS 400 POUNDS (181 KG). But remember the power of the pack: Multiply 400 times the number of wolves. **YIKES!**

Wolves are found in lots of different habitats. They're at home in forests, prairies, deserts, and even the frigid tundra—pretty much any place with food!

BITE BUSINESS

If gray wolves had a motto, it would probably be: "Power of the pack, baby! Power of the pack!" Wolves live and hunt together in large groups, called packs, of 20 to 30 members. They live and die by the strength of their pack. **Pack members work together** to chase down their prey, which can be as large as a half-ton (.45-t) moose! When the prey gets tired and stops, the wolves immediately circle around it, darting in and biting the animal on the rump (the less dangerous end). Eventually, the prey dies from massive blood loss, and the pack goes to work feeding.

A hungry pack can make quick work of even a large carcass—because they have the **right eating utensils** for it! Wolves have specialized teeth that perform different tasks. Their large canines can hang on to prey or slice through arteries. The incisors up front nip and snip meat. The premolars, called carnassials, are powerful meat shears that carve up prey. The flat molars in the back of the mouth crack bones. All these specialty teeth enable wolves to eat a wide variety of things, from moose to berries and nuts.

1 2 3 BY THE NUMBERS

WOLVES HAVE 42 SPECIALIZED TEETH: 20 TOP AND 22 BOTTOM. Their canine teeth are two inches (5 cm) long. Grandma, what BIG teeth you have!

TIGER SHARK

BITE FORCE

THE TIGER SHARK'S 400-POUND (181-KG) bite force equals the weight of two manhole covers. That's not much for its size—about the same as a wolf's.

MEET *THE BEAST*

THE TIGER SHARK IS NO JUNGLE CAT. It's named for the tigerlike stripes along its body, which are most prominent in young sharks and fade with age. When grown, a tiger shark is about the same size as a great white shark. It measures around 18 feet (5.5 m) long and weighs a ton (0.9 t). **That's a big shark!** And its broad, boxy-looking head has a wider mouth than most sharks. It's perfect for stuffing in lots of food!

WHAT'S ON THE
MENU

TIGER SHARKS are often called the "garbage collectors" of the sea. Just about everything has been found in their stomachs! Their unique teeth and biting strategy allow them to devour hard-bodied prey that other sharks cannot. As a result, just about the whole sea is on the menu. They have been known to eat **fish, seabirds, snakes, other sharks, stingrays, dolphins, squid,** and even hard-shelled **sea turtles.** They are also known man-eaters, so steer clear!

SEA TURTLE

DID YOU KNOW?

LICENSE PLATES AND CAR TIRES have been found in tiger shark stomachs! (You'd think they were eating cars!)

A group of sharks together like this is called a shiver of sharks. This shiver's checking out a bait box we put out.

TOOTH

BITE BUSINESS

Think of the tiger shark as the saw-jaw, thanks to its unique, unmistakable teeth. Its teeth act like tiny specialized saw blades that cut and saw through prey. Each of its short, wide teeth has a large point, or cusp, in the middle with serrations on both sides. The front edge has lots of fine serrations that make it razor sharp—perfect for cutting. The serrations behind the cusp are larger and heavier, like the **teeth on a big saw.**

The tiger shark doesn't have a very **strong bite** for such a large shark, but it doesn't need one, thanks to these special teeth and the way it uses them. First the shark gets a grip on its hard-shelled prey, such as a sea turtle, by sinking in its teeth. Then it swings its loosely attached upper jaw side to side in a sawing motion. That makes quick work of even the hardest prey. Sawing through a turtle shell can be tough business; the shark may lose teeth during the process. But it has numerous rows of replacement teeth ready to move into position for the next sawing project.

123 BY THE NUMBERS

THEIR **48 FRONT-ROW TEETH** are identical on the top and bottom. They measure an inch (2.5 cm) long and less than an inch high.

GHARIAL

MEET THE BEAST

THE GHARIAL IS ONE OF THE LONGEST crocodilians on the planet. It can grow to more than **20 feet** (6.1 m) long! For all other crocodilians, the males and females look alike. But for gharials, the male has a big bulbous knot, called a ghara, on the tip of its nose. Its snout is also the longest and narrowest of any croc, and its toothy grin is filled with lots of sharp teeth.

DID YOU KNOW?

GHARIALS, LIKE ALL CROCODILIANS, must swallow their food above the water's surface to avoid drowning.

BITE FORCE

THIS MASSIVE CROC'S BITE FORCE is around 200 pounds (91 kg). It may not sound like much, but it's plenty for snagging slimy fish.

MENU

Fish, fish, and more fish: It's on the menu every day for these fish specialists. The **GHARIAL'S** slender jaws are not designed for taking down hard-bodied prey like turtles or strong struggling prey like mammals. At times they will eat small crustaceans, like **crabs and shrimps.** (Maybe it's to break up the monotony of fish, fish, and more fish!) Small gharials have a more extensive diet. They will prey upon **insects, snails,** and amphibians like **frogs and tadpoles.** But otherwise: Fish! Get your fresh fish here!

CRAB

BITE BUSINESS

The gharial's long, narrow snout is lined with interlocking teeth. They make a **perfect fish trap**—and that's a good thing when you're a fish-eater! The teeth are all about the same size, narrow, and slightly recurved, all good things for gripping. The narrow snout can slice through the water with little resistance. That extra speed is great for gharials because fish are fast, and if you want to catch them, you need to be even faster! Gharials can snap side to side with blinding speed—less than one-fifth of a second. That's the same speed as a blink of an eye!

Gharials also have a secret weapon for locating fish in muddy water. They have tiny **motion receptors** along their jaws that detect fish movement. They act like radar in the water, helping gharials find prey and letting them know when to snap!

1 2 3 BY THE NUMBERS

THE GHARIAL HAS OVER 100 SLENDER, interlocking, needle-sharp teeth. These replaceable teeth are all similar in appearance along the entire length of the jaw.

Brady's BITE Story

Surprise, Surprise!

HAVE YOU HEARD OF THE HEIMLICH MANEUVER?

It is a way of trying to help someone who is choking. You grab that person around the middle from behind, kind of like you're hugging them. You quickly squeeze his or her belly in an upward motion to try to force whatever's stuck in the throat to come shooting out.

Well, believe it or not, it works with alligators, too! The move is used not to save them from choking, but to find out what they have been eating. First, you hold the alligator's mouth open with a piece of plastic pipe, and then fill its stomach with water. You squeeze with all your might, just like when you're doing the Heimlich maneuver. Everything comes up and is caught in a big plastic tub. Peee-eww! It smells terrible when the stuff comes up! **But it's important to know what gators eat.** It helps scientists like me know how to protect them better.

I have performed the Heimlich maneuver on more than 1,000 alligators. I've seen just about everything vomited up: birds, fish, turtles, snakes, cans, flip-flops, fishing lures, trash, you name it! However, a few years ago, I squeezed something out of a gator's stomach that still leaves me shaking my head in complete amazement.

I was in the Florida Everglades. It was late at night, and I had just captured an alligator. I placed it across my lap and was giving it the Heimlich. My plastic tub was under the gator's mouth to catch its food. I was squeezing and hugging that big gator with all my might. Stuff started coming out of the stomach: fish, lots of snails, and some unidentified blob.

Then, in a flash, I saw something else, something furry and brown. Lots of times I see mammals come out of a gator's stomach—things like rats, rabbits, and deer. One time I even got a bobcat (well, pieces of a bobcat). This time, the furry object flew out of the gator's mouth so quickly I didn't get a chance to see what it was. I leaned down to look in my tub: It was an otter! But it wasn't just a piece of an otter. It was the whole thing, and this otter was looking back at me! That's right, looking at me! It sneezed, shook its head once or twice, then jumped out of the tub, over the side of the boat, and swam away. It was alive!

Man, I couldn't believe it. The alligator must have just swallowed it right before I came along. Gators don't chew their food. They swallow it whole or rip it into pieces that they can swallow. My big old gator must have swallowed that otter whole, and then a few minutes later I squeezed it right back out. **That was the luckiest otter on the planet!** He got swallowed by a gator and lived to tell about it. And I didn't even get a thank-you!

I always take careful scientific measurements of alligators so that I can learn as much about the animal as possible.

Sometimes capturing wily old alligators involves leaving the safety of the airboat and wading into the water to come face to face with them on their turf!

Airboats are like airplanes without wings! They're designed to operate in shallow water and are powered by a giant propeller that sits right behind your head. Yikes!

JAGUAR

MEET THE BEAST

THE JAGUAR IS THE LARGEST CAT IN THE AMERICAS, at more than six feet (1.8 m) long and more than 100 pounds (45 kg). This compact, muscular jungle cat has short, powerful legs and a big boxy head (big biter clue). Dark rosettes (spots that resemble roses) adorn its coat, which ranges from light colored to all black—handy camouflage for this nighttime hunter. **They hang out in trees,** so lock up your tree house!

DID YOU KNOW?

JAGUARS CAN BITE right through the armored skin of crocodiles.

JAGUARS HAVE 30 TEETH, almost as many as you. Their 1.5-inch (3.8-cm) supersharp canines are made for piercing skulls!

·••·• WHAT'S ON THE •·••·
MENU

Researchers have found that **JAGUARS** eat more than 80 different types of prey. Talk about a jungle buffet! They eat not only big animals like **tapirs, peccaries,** and **deer,** but also smaller creatures like **armadillos, squirrels,** and **lizards.** They also eat things that you might not suspect. Jaguars love the water. When the mood hits them, they are really good at grabbing an aquatic snack such as **crocodiles, caimans, fish,** and even **sea turtles.** Jags love their surf and turf menu!

TAPIR

BITE BUSINESS

Jaguars can be thought of as **death from above,** because of their habit of dropping down from trees onto unsuspecting prey. Their powerful jaws and specialized teeth make this cat a unique killer. Other big cats take down prey with a bite to the throat, a powerful swat to the head, or a bite to the back of the neck. But the jaguar goes for a head bite! That's right, a bite to the skull, the hardest part of the animal! Seems crazy, right? It kills with a bite to the victim's temples to pierce the brain. It's not easy, but the jaguar pulls it off with supersharp canines and a humongous bite. Its shorter jaws provide more force and leverage up front, where the canines are. That combination makes jaguars one of the real heavy hitters in the big-bite club! This ability also allows the jaguar to bite through the hard shells of turtles, prey that most jungle predators just couldn't tackle. **It's one of the strongest biters on the planet—**something you might want to remember if you ever go tree climbing in the jungle!

BITE FORCE

RESEARCHERS HAVE MEASURED the jaguar's bite force to be a whopping one ton (0.9 t)! That equals a speedboat's weight on top of the jaws.

NILE CROCODILE

MEET THE BEAST

THE NILE CROCODILE is one of the planet's largest predators at more than 20 feet (6.1 m) long and weighing almost 2,000 pounds (907 kg). The toothy end isn't the only dangerous part of the croc. The extremely powerful tail can be **used as a weapon.** Bony plates called osteoderms cover the body and protect the animal like a suit of armor. I have found bullets lodged in osteoderms! This is one tough beast.

BITE FORCE

THE CROC IS THE PLANET'S STRONGEST BITER with more than 5,000 pounds (2,270 kg) of bite force. That's like having a rhinoceros's weight on top of its jaws!

CHOWING DOWN ON AN IMPALA

BITE BUSINESS

The Nile croc uses a chomp, chomp, and roll feeding strategy. (This is not to be confused with the stop, drop, and roll strategy used if you are on fire!) Crocs don't chew their food; their teeth aren't designed for it. They must **gulp prey whole** or tear off pieces they can swallow. They grab prey with their mighty jaws, which are powered by massive muscles that lock the jaws shut. Then they hold on tight. Crocs will usually drown their prey; they can hold their breath for hours underwater if needed. Then it's chow time! They hold prey fast with their jaws and use their powerful tail to spin or roll, sometimes called the death roll. That maneuver rips off a piece of prey. Sometimes crocs will work together, holding on tight and spinning in opposite directions to tear a meal apart. With the **strongest bite on the planet,** crocs frequently break teeth. Not to worry: They have new teeth growing from below existing teeth. The teeth are hollow and stacked on top of each other, just like you would stack plastic cups.

1 2 3 BY THE NUMBERS

NILE CROCS HAVE AROUND 68 HOLLOW, replaceable, needle-sharp teeth. The fourth lower tooth is oversize and sticks above the upper lip.

• • • • WHAT'S ON THE • • • •
MENU

Large and small, hard and soft— just about anything the **CROC** can sink its teeth into is on the menu. It eats everything from **fish, turtles, snakes, lizards,** and even **snails,** to large prey like **wildebeests, zebras,** and other hooved mammals. Anything that comes to the water's edge for a drink could be the daily special. Sometimes crocs use their powerful tails to propel themselves straight out of the water like a missile to grab **monkeys, bats,** or **roosting birds** right out of trees!

DID YOU KNOW?

CROCS CAN'T DIGEST HAIR. They have to hack up hair balls just like your pet cat.

Family Portrait

CROCODILIANS

THE CROCODILIAN FAMILY IS SMALL—VERY SMALL. There are only 24 species. Compare that to the snake family, with around 3,000 known species, or the more than 900,000 insect species!

"Crocodilian" is a funny word. It doesn't mean just the 15 species of crocodiles. There are other members of the crocodilian family as well: alligators (two species), caimans (six species) and the gharial (one species). The big question is: Since the family is so small—and its members share so many similarities—how in the world do you tell these different branches of the crocodile family tree apart?

African Slender-Snouted Crocodile

Crocodiles like the African slender-snouted crocodile have pointed noses that are great for slashing through the water and catching prey.

Spectacled Caiman

Caimans like the spectacled caiman have wide, round snouts, kind of like a duck's bill. (So do alligators.) It's good for cracking bones and turtle shells.

Mugger Crocodile

Like all crocodiles, the mugger crocodile shows its upper and lower teeth when its mouth is closed. (Its name comes from a Hindi word for "water monster.")

Chinese Alligator

Alligators like this Chinese alligator only show their upper teeth if their mouth is closed. What nice pearly whites you have!

Siamese Crocodile

Like all crocs, the Siamese crocodile has one of the strongest bites on the planet. But its muscles for opening its mouth are so weak that you could hold its mouth shut with just one hand.

Sarcosuchus

Sarcosuchus was a croc that lived 112 million years ago. It had teeth that were larger than your hand and used them to eat dinosaurs!

Cuban Crocodile

The Cuban crocodile has large bones on the top of its skull that make it look like the croc has horns.

AFRICAN WILD DOG

MEET THE BEAST

AFRICAN WILD DOGS HAVE A STUNNINGLY COLORED mottled coat that looks like someone threw cans of paint on them. Their coat has splotches of red, brown, yellow, and black. They are one of the most beautiful animals around, but they're no wimps. **They are lean, mean hunting machines!** Their tall build and long legs make them look like distance runners, but they're built for both endurance and speed.

BITE FORCE

AFRICAN WILD DOGS HAVE A BITE FORCE of more than 300 pounds (136 kg). That's like the weight of 30 bowling balls pressing down on their jaws!

1 2 3 BY THE NUMBERS

THEY HAVE 42 TEETH—same as your pet dog—but their canines are skinnier than your dog's. The last molar is greatly undersized, while the premolars are huge.

BITE BUSINESS

African wild dogs are the speed demons of the predator world. They hunt fast and definitely eat fast. Hunting parties chase down prey by exhausting it. When the prey stops, the dogs don't kill with a neck bite to suffocate or paralyze like big cats do. Instead, these dogs grab hold of the tired animal and tear it apart. Many times they start feeding before the prey is even dead ... **Yikes!**

Their teeth are specially designed to make quick work of a kill. They have one lower molar on each side of the jaw that has a tall slicing blade. This is called a trenchant heel. It allows the dogs to slice through meat extra fast. Their canines are long and skinny for chomping and holding on to prey. Their premolars are oversize for cracking bone. Unlike your mom, wild dog mothers don't tell their kids to slow down and enjoy their meal. The dogs eat their meal quickly and hit the road, moving on before other predators and scavengers arrive at the kill. Eating fast and moving on to avoid fights with competitors is a smart way to stay safe. For these dogs, **fast food is a good thing!**

WHAT'S ON THE
MENU

Medium-size hooved mammals dominate the **AFRICAN WILD DOG'S** menu. Their favorite eats include **antelope**, **impala**, **ostrich**, **gazelle**, and **waterbuck**. They will also dine on **warthogs**, **small birds**, and even **rodents** on occasion, but they prefer larger game. Wild dogs hunt twice a day—once in the morning and again in the evening—to keep the pack healthy and happy. They are such successful hunters that they rarely have to scavenge carcasses. They're also well-mannered dining partners, never fighting or squabbling over a kill like hyenas and lions do.

DID **YOU** KNOW?

AFRICAN WILD DOGS MAKE KILLS on about 80 percent of their hunts, making them one of the most efficient and successful predators on the planet!

TYRANNOSAURUS REX

MEET THE BEAST

YOU'VE SEEN THE MUG SHOT. Thirteen feet (3.9 m) tall, 40 feet (12.2 m) long, and weighing in at six tons (5.4 t), its jaw is longer than your arm and is filled with razor-sharp teeth the size of railroad spikes! I don't know about you, but I'm glad the *T. rex* is extinct!

···· WHAT'S ON THE
M E N U

We don't know for sure what *T. REX* ate, but scientists study fossil clues to try and solve the mystery. When you have a huge head, and jaws armed with massive serrated teeth, it's safe to say that you are a meat-eater! However, it's not known for sure whether *T. rex* was a scavenger, hunter, or a little bit of both. Regardless, it likely had the jaw power and teeth to pierce the armor of most dinosaurs out there. One thing we do know: As one of the heaviest of the heavyweights, *T. rex* no doubt ate a lot!

1·2·3 BY THE NUMBERS

TYRANNOSAURUS REX HAD MORE THAN 60 LONG, SERRATED, REPLACE-ABLE TEETH. The largest were around 10 to 12 inches (25 to 30 cm) long, the biggest teeth of any carnivorous dinosaur.

BITE FORCE

BITE BUSINESS

Tyrannosaurus rex was definitely designed for **power biting.** It had a mouth full of specialized teeth. The chisel-like front teeth were packed tightly together. The serrated side teeth—flesh rippers—were spaced farther apart. The back teeth were designed for carving. The *T. rex* used those chompers to bite down on thick-skinned dinosaurs, so its teeth had to not only be sharp but also durable. Its teeth had extra layers of dentine, the same stuff that makes your teeth strong. This made the *T. rex*'s teeth super tough, so it could easily crunch through the toughest meals.

These deadly teeth were housed in a massive skull that was designed for power. A *T. rex*'s skull was more than **five feet** (1.5 m) **long** and had huge openings in the back for giant biting muscles. On top was a long ridge called a sagittal crest, where the biting muscles attached. Parts of the skull were even designed like a honeycomb, making it extra strong to withstand the forces of big bites. And for those big bites, it could open its jaws almost **90 degrees** to get a good grip and maximize damage. No wonder *T. rex* is called the king of dinosaurs!

DID YOU KNOW?

T. REX WASN'T THE LARGEST meat-eating dinosaur. That honor went to *Spinosaurus*, 55 feet (16.8 m) and eight tons (7.3 t) of bone-crunching terror!

SPOTTED HYENA

MEET THE BEAST

THIS SPOTTED BEAST is one strange-looking customer. It kind of looks like a dog, but it's more closely related to a cat. It looks like it has been pumping iron, because of its bulked-up front end. It has a thick, muscled neck and a huge head with large ears. It stands three feet (1 m) tall and can weigh almost 200 pounds (91 kg), making it the **second largest carnivore** in Africa, behind the lion.

BITE FORCE

ITS 1,000-POUND (454-KG) BITE FORCE is one of the greatest in the animal kingdom. That's the weight of about 1,400 cans of soda!

POOP

DID YOU KNOW?

HYENAS EAT so many bones that their poop is white!

THEIR 34 TEETH ARE HIGHLY MODIFIED FOR CRACKING BONES— especially the premolars, which are the largest of all carnivores.

BITE BUSINESS

Hyenas would have no problem making quick work of even the biggest jawbreaker candy, because they are bone-cracking specialists. That bone-snapping ability all starts with the skull. Their skulls are designed for power and strength, much more so than other carnivores. They have a big ridge, called a sagittal crest, that runs across the top of their skull. This ridge is where the powerful biting muscles (temporalis) attach to the skull. Whenever you see a large sagittal crest on an animal's skull, it is a good clue that the animal has big-time bite force.

To go along with its tanklike skull are some highly specialized teeth that are designed—you guessed it—for power. The short, stocky canine teeth stand up to struggling prey and rip meat from a carcass. The oversize premolars are designed for bone cracking. They're **similar to a nutcracker** you might use to break open walnuts. All of these characteristics allow hyenas to eat parts of prey—like the bones—that other predators can't eat and leave behind.

WHAT'S ON THE
MENU

Just about any animal on the savanna is on the menu for **HYENAS**. They'll devour larger prey like **hippos, warthogs, wildebeests, antelope, African buffalo,** and **zebras** (really, any grazing mammal), but they'll also eat small **birds** and **lizards**. They are skilled hunters and have even been known to tackle **rhinos!** Still, they'll never pass up the opportunity for an easy meal by scavenging or stealing. They're the master thieves of the animal kingdom. They're so good at pilfering food from **lions, leopards,** and **cheetahs** that those big cats should have the police on speed dial!

TRAP-JAW ANT

MEET THE BEAST

THIS ANT LOOKS LIKE IT HAS A BEAR TRAP strapped to the front of its face. The trap is actually the ant's humongous mandibles, or jaws, that it uses to grab prey. These ants aren't big; you could fit a bunch of them onto a single penny. Don't let their size fool you. These puny ants pack one **powerful bite** up front, and a venomous sting at the back!

A trap-jaw ant hangs upside down with its mandibles open, ready to snap shut on unsuspecting prey.

BITE FORCE

THE BITE FORCE IS ABOUT A HUNDREDTH OF A POUND (4.5 g). But remember: The ant weighs only 10 milligrams—about the same as 10 of your eyelashes!

32

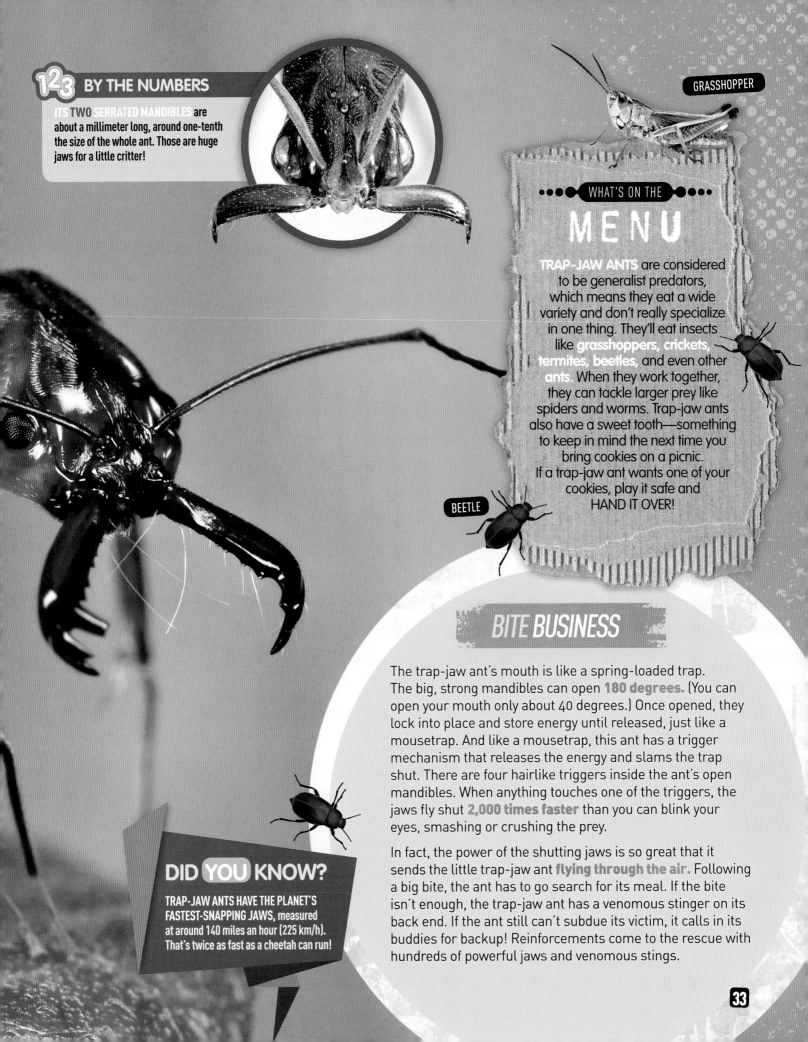

ITS TWO SERRATED MANDIBLES are about a millimeter long, around one-tenth the size of the whole ant. Those are huge jaws for a little critter!

GRASSHOPPER

•••• WHAT'S ON THE ••••
MENU

TRAP-JAW ANTS are considered to be generalist predators, which means they eat a wide variety and don't really specialize in one thing. They'll eat insects like grasshoppers, crickets, termites, beetles, and even other ants. When they work together, they can tackle larger prey like spiders and worms. Trap-jaw ants also have a sweet tooth—something to keep in mind the next time you bring cookies on a picnic. If a trap-jaw ant wants one of your cookies, play it safe and HAND IT OVER!

BEETLE

BITE BUSINESS

The trap-jaw ant's mouth is like a spring-loaded trap. The big, strong mandibles can open **180 degrees.** (You can open your mouth only about 40 degrees.) Once opened, they lock into place and store energy until released, just like a mousetrap. And like a mousetrap, this ant has a trigger mechanism that releases the energy and slams the trap shut. There are four hairlike triggers inside the ant's open mandibles. When anything touches one of the triggers, the jaws fly shut **2,000 times faster** than you can blink your eyes, smashing or crushing the prey.

In fact, the power of the shutting jaws is so great that it sends the little trap-jaw ant **flying through the air.** Following a big bite, the ant has to go search for its meal. If the bite isn't enough, the trap-jaw ant has a venomous stinger on its back end. If the ant still can't subdue its victim, it calls in its buddies for backup! Reinforcements come to the rescue with hundreds of powerful jaws and venomous stings.

DID YOU KNOW?

TRAP-JAW ANTS HAVE THE PLANET'S FASTEST-SNAPPING JAWS, measured at around 140 miles an hour (225 km/h). That's twice as fast as a cheetah can run!

CHAPTER 2

SLICERS

These next beasts are all equipped with something like a fine set of steak knives in their mouths. Their teeth are SHARP, PRECISE, AND DANGEROUS, making them experts at slicing and dicing their way through prey.

Mystery Bite

NOT LONG AGO, I was slogging through a Florida swamp at night looking for salamanders. Wading around in a swamp is always unnerving, but wading around in a swamp at night can be plain scary. You never know what's lurking below the murky surface. I knew that the biggest danger I faced was not from alligators but from venomous snakes, so I was wearing my favorite rubber boots that are 100 percent effective against snakebites. Most animals cannot bite through the thick rubber, so I felt extra safe in those boots.

I had been wading around for hours with my headlamp on and hadn't seen a single salamander, gator, or snake. In fact, I hadn't seen anything. I was ready to quit and head home when it happened. Out of nowhere, **WHAM!** Something hit me. It felt like I had been kicked hard in the back of my leg. Something had bitten me!

I was knocked off my feet and into the dark waters. **"AGGGGHHH, ALLIGATOR!"** I screamed. I staggered to shore. Something had bitten right through my trusted boot! My leg was okay, but the boot had a strangely shaped hole. It didn't look like a gator bite.

I had to know what it was that had bitten me. Was it a new kind of gator? I grabbed a long stick and started poking around in the water, but there was nothing there.

It was a mystery. I poked some more: Still nothing. I felt only the muddy, rocky bottom. What could it be? I was baffled.

I poked with the stick one last time, and this time I felt something moving. I recognized the swirling motion and knew immediately what had bitten me. I plunged my arm underwater and felt a gnarled tail. I clutched it and pulled out a humongous alligator snapping turtle! **The huge fella looked like a dinosaur.**

The mystery was solved, but now I had a new task: to find some better boots that are 100 percent effective against turtle bites!

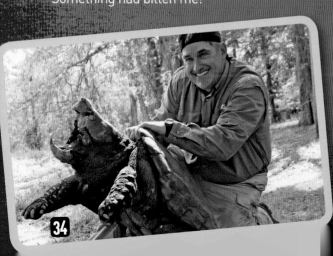

ALLIGATOR SNAPPING TURTLE

THE ALLIGATOR SNAPPING TURTLE (or gator snapper, as its friends call it) is a massive turtle. It grows to **200 POUNDS** (91 kg), making it one of the largest freshwater turtles in the world. It has a grouchy attitude and is armed with a huge head, sharp beak, and powerful bite. No wonder so few animals—friend or foe—tangle with the gator snapper!

DID YOU KNOW?

THEY'RE CALLED SNAPPING TURTLES FOR A REASON: The gator snapper can snap a wooden broom handle in two with its powerful beak.

AN ALLIGATOR SNAPPING TURTLE'S CHOMP has been measured at over 1,000 pounds (454 kg). That's more powerful than a lion's. (Take that, king of beasts!)

BITE FORCE

WHAT'S ON THE

MENU

This brute is both a hunter and a scavenger. It will eat just about anything living or dead, plant or animal. The **GATOR SNAPPER'S** menu often includes **fish, other turtles, snakes, small mammals, birds, acorns,** and **vegetation.** Its powerful jaws and sharp beak can make quick work of anything that it decides should be food. (Fingers crossed it's not your foot!)

BITE BUSINESS

Do you like to go fishing? So does the gator snapper, but it fishes a little differently than you. The turtle lies very still on the bottom of a river and holds its mouth wide open, setting a trap for an unsuspecting fish. For its bait, the turtle uses a small, light-colored piece of skin on its tongue that looks just like a wiggling worm. The snapper moves the bait back and forth until a fish swims in to grab a worm snack. Before the fish realizes something fishy is going on—**WHAM!**—the turtle slams shut its strong hooked beak. The turtle's powerful jaws hang on tight to the fish—if the slicing beak didn't already cut it in two. The turtle then shears off pieces to swallow or sucks down the fish whole. Plus there's one bonus for the alligator snapper: **It never runs out of bait!**

1 2 3 BY THE NUMBERS

THE GATOR SNAPPER HAS ZERO TEETH. But it can still bite with the best of them, thanks to its strong jaw muscles and sharp beak.

GREAT WHITE SHARK

MEET THE BEAST

WHEN THE WORD "GREAT" IS IN YOUR NAME, you must be special. This fish is the rock star of the shark world: It's big, bold, and confident. It is the biggest predatory fish on Earth, growing to 20 feet (6.1 m) long and tipping the scales at two tons (1.8 t). **That's around the weight of an SUV!** They are found where ocean temperatures range between 55 and 75 degrees Fahrenheit (13–24 degrees Celsius)—so watch out!

BITE BUSINESS

Meet the **"bite and spit"** predator. The great white attacks at high speed to cut and slice with a huge bite. Then it spits out dinner, cruises off, and waits awhile before returning to feed. It's safer that way; no need to take a chance being injured by struggling prey. When it's ready to eat, its mouth is armed with big razor-sharp teeth that are constantly replaced. The upper teeth are serrated like a steak knife and are used for cutting. The lower teeth are narrower and are used for stabbing.

Among the great white's **deadly bag of tricks** is its protrusible jaw. "Protrusible" means that it can extend forward. When the shark bites, it extends its protrusible jaws and pops them out of its mouth like a crazy set of false teeth. This provides a bigger mouth for a bigger mouthful!

Sometimes the great white attacks its prey from below at great speeds. It can even breach, or launch itself completely out of the water! The ramming force of a great white is powerful enough to knock a sea lion unconscious. In fact, it's so powerful it has been measured at more than **12 times the force** that astronauts feel on rocket liftoff!

BITE FORCE

I'VE MEASURED A GREAT WHITE'S bite force at over 600 pounds (272.4 kg). That's about the weight of a big motorcycle!

DID YOU KNOW?

IT'S BEEN ESTIMATED THAT A GREAT WHITE SHARK goes through 50,000 teeth in its lifetime. (Humans go through a measly 52 in comparison.)

Here I am, measuring the bite force of a great white. The dynamometer, or bite-force meter, is covered in a mesh bag filled with fish.

ACTUAL SIZE

1 2 3 BY THE NUMBERS

GREAT WHITES HAVE ABOUT 48 EXPOSED TEETH, with hundreds of replacement teeth in waiting. Its largest teeth are 2.5 inches (6.3 cm) long.

WHAT'S ON THE

MENU

So you don't like to eat your carrots? **GREAT WHITE SHARKS** are picky eaters too. Even though they're thought of as eating machines, they concentrate on specific types of prey. They prefer fatty mammals like **seals, sea lions, porpoises, or even whales.** (They love a whale blubber lunch!) Some researchers think that great whites don't attack humans more frequently because we're lower in body fat compared to seals. Now there's a great reason to eat healthy!

BLACK PIRANHA

1-2-3 BY THE NUMBERS

A PIRANHA HAS ABOUT 24 TEETH. It has a single row of small triangular teeth (smaller than a half inch [1.3 cm]), each one with three sharp points.

MEET THE BEAST

THE BLACK PIRANHA IS A SHORT, stocky fish that measures only around a foot (0.3 m) long. What it lacks in size, it makes up for in attitude! It has a fierce reputation, and its bulldog-like underbite and wicked teeth give it a real tough-guy appearance. The black piranha is found in freshwaters of the Amazon Basin of South America. **They should definitely post a "no swimming" sign there!**

WHAT'S ON THE MENU

A **BLACK PIRANHA** usually eats lots of **fish**, **crustaceans**, **insects**, and **amphibians**, pretty much anything that swims by. Occasionally it will munch on a small animal that falls into the water. As a school, piranhas will feast on significantly larger prey—such as a **capybara**—that is dead or dying. When there's not a lot of food around, piranhas have been known to take a bite out of other **piranhas**. (Hey, a fish has got to eat!)

CAPYBARA

40

BITE FORCE

BITE BUSINESS

You've probably heard that cooperation is a good thing. It's good for piranhas, too. They are cooperative predators, meaning that they work together to bring down prey much larger than themselves. It's death by a thousand bites.

In a large school they can be a nightmare, but even alone one piranha can be a really bad dream. Each piranha is **armed with razor-sharp, replaceable teeth** that are perfect for carving meat. They don't replace their teeth individually like sharks, but in sets, a quarter of their teeth at a time. Their teeth interlock, just like your fingers when you hold your hands together. This provides piranhas more strength and stability during a big bite.

In fact, big bite is an understatement; piranhas have a humongous bite! For its size, this fish has the **strongest bite** of any fish on the planet. This power comes from supersized jaw muscles that take up most of its head, and the unique closing design of the lower jaw. Put it all together, and the piranha is a perfectly designed aquatic chomping machine.

DID YOU KNOW?

A RECENT STUDY SHOWED the bite of a piranha is about three times stronger than an alligator of the same size. See ya later, alligator!

KOMODO DRAGON

MEET *THE BEAST*

THE KOMODO DRAGON MIGHT BE THE ULTIMATE PREDATOR. It's big, fast, strong, and tough! At more than 10 feet (3 m) long and 300 pounds (136 kg), it's the world's largest lizard. Tiny bones embedded in its skin, called osteoderms, **protect the dragon like armor.** Its heavily muscled limbs are tipped with sharp tearing claws. Its long snout is armed with replaceable scalpel-like teeth that inflict a venomous bite. And surprisingly, it can run super fast!

1²3 BY THE NUMBERS

EVEN THEIR TEETH HAVE TEETH!
A Komodo dragon's **60 teeth** are around an inch (2.5 cm) long. These flat, highly serrated recurved teeth look like tiny scalpels.

DID **YOU** KNOW?

A KOMODO DRAGON AND ADULT HUMAN have about the same bite force. But the dragon takes down huge water buffalo, whereas we take down Buffalo wings!

WHAT'S ON THE
MENU

If it's meat, **DRAGONS** eat it! They eat anything they catch or find, from **mice** to **lizards**, **birds** to **water buffalo**. They are also known cannibals. When dragons are young and small, they avoid being eaten by other dragons by living in trees, where they catch a lot of **insects** and **lizards**. In addition to hunting prey, Komodo dragons are also scavengers. They can smell rotting meat from more than two miles (3.2 km) away! No matter what they're eating, they waste very little. They'll gobble up hooves, bone, hide—just about everything! They're definitely members of the clean-plate club.

BITE BUSINESS

Komodo dragons are sit-and-wait predators. That means they like to launch deadly surprise attacks on unsuspecting big prey, like a half-ton (.45-t) water buffalo. Here's how they pull it off: Their razor-sharp teeth are recurved, which means they bend backward. The backside of their teeth is highly serrated, like a saw blade. Their teeth are **similar to those of some dinosaurs,** like velociraptors, and are perfectly designed for delivering huge fatal wounds.

Once its teeth slice in and are locked into its prey, the dragon uses its powerful neck muscles to pull and shake, just like a pet dog playing with its chew toy. The dragon's thrashing opens up massive wounds, where its deadly drool can go to work. **Dragons are venomous,** so even a small bite can be fatal. They don't have a strong bite force, but they do have a unique skull that is flexible in places, similar to a snake. This enables the dragon to take larger bites and provides more leverage for those slicing teeth to do their damage. Maybe it's a good thing Komodo dragons are found only on a few islands in Indonesia!

BITE FORCE

ITS BITE FORCE HAS BEEN MEASURED AT ABOUT 163 POUNDS (74 KG), about the weight of a toilet. That's not much for such a giant lizard.

43

Brady's BITE Story

KOMODO DRAGON

Have You Ever Been Chased by a Dragon?

IF YOU THINK THAT DRAGONS ARE ONLY FOUND IN FAIRY TALES, YOU'RE WRONG!

Dragons are definitely real. How do I know? I've been chased by one—a Komodo dragon, that is. They are alive and well on four islands in the Asian country of Indonesia.

Komodo dragons are extremely dangerous. They're about the size of a refrigerator and have long powerful tails, sharp claws, and knife-edged teeth. Oh, and don't forget that they're venomous, too! One nip can be deadly.

A few years ago I traveled to Komodo Island to take part in a scientific study. **We wanted to determine the dragons' strength, speed, and bite force.** I was super excited, but I also was scared because I knew how dangerous dragons could be.

I thought that getting close to a dragon to measure its bite force would be the most dangerous experiment. But the experiments turned out to be pretty easy, except for one: the test for speed. I didn't believe the dragon experts when they told me their plan to measure how fast the dragons could run. They wanted to tie pieces of meat on strings and tie the strings to my belt. Then they'd have me run and let the dragons chase me and my meat tail! They would clock the speed of the running dragons with a radar gun.

I didn't like that plan at all! **What if I fell down and the dragons caught me?** Yikes! When the scientists tied the meat to my belt, I thought of backing out of the crazy test. Suddenly, a big dragon raced toward me! Now I had no choice. The experiment was under way!

I took off like a shot. I could hear the Komodo dragon's hot breath and its sharp claws hitting the ground right behind me. I thought I heard the dragon snapping its jaws as it pictured having me as its early lunch. I'm normally a slow runner, but that thought made me run for my life.

By now, other dragons had joined the hunt. I had a whole pack of hungry dragons chasing after me! The speed guns recorded their speed at almost 25 miles an hour (40.2 km/h). Whoa—

I never knew I could run that fast!

The plan worked perfectly, except for one small detail: How do we get the dragons to stop chasing me?! They had no "off" button. Everyone was screaming. No one knew what to do. It was chaos.

I suddenly had a bright idea. I quickly climbed up a tree where the big Komodo dragons couldn't follow. Whew, I was finally safe!

The next time someone asks if **dragons are real,** you can say, "Yes." Because believe me, they definitely are—definitely real and definitely fast!

Komodo is the largest island that the dragons call home. It's part of a group of islands called the Lesser Sunda Islands in Southeast Asia. Sometimes the dragons swim from island to island.

These dragons may look harmless but parts of their venom are as toxic as the most venomous snake.

HUMBOLDT SQUID

MEET THE BEAST

AT FIVE FEET (1.5 M) LONG AND 100 POUNDS (45 kg), the Humboldt squid is a jumbo! It has no skeleton, so its body is completely soft, except for its hard, slicing beak. It has two long, retractable tentacles used for grabbing, with suckers on their clublike ends. Its **eight arms** are covered with powerful suckers ringed with sharp teeth. Add large eyes and a sharp intelligence, and you have one scary sea monster!

1²3 BY THE NUMBERS

ITS EIGHT ARMS have more than 40,000 small, sharp teeth that are used for grasping. Its powerful cutting beak is the size of your fist.

DID YOU KNOW?

HUMBOLDT SQUID are one of the fastest-growing animals. They start out the size of a grain of rice and reach five feet (1.5 m) in two years.

WHAT'S ON THE
MENU

JUMBO SQUID are often called red devils or cannibal squid. (You can guess the reason behind the last nickname: They sometimes eat each other!) These intelligent and aggressive pack hunters cruise in large groups called shoals that can number more than a thousand squid. They hunt the depths for **krill, fish, shrimps, and mollusks.** And lanternfish are definitely a favorite.

LANTERNFISH

BITE BUSINESS

These pack hunters are super aggressive, which makes them your worst nightmare if you are a fish. Once a squid spots its prey with its giant eyes, it sneaks up silently and swiftly, swimming as fast as 20 miles an hour (32.2 km/h). Before its prey can react, the squid grabs it with its long tentacles and pulls it quickly within reach of the eight writhing arms. The thousands of tiny teeth circling the arms' suckers hold the fish tight as the squid stuffs it ever closer to its mouth and its snapping razor-sharp beak. The beak is located atop what looks like a tiny elephant trunk. That flexible "trunk" lets the beak shoot out, pull back, and swivel in any direction to deal out destruction. **Powerful muscles make the beak super strong—**strong enough to even shear through bones! Inside the mouth is a rough tongue called a radula, which is covered in microscopic teeth. The radula further grinds food that the beak cuts up, like making a smoothie in a blender!

BEAK

THIS SOFT-BODIED SQUID has an unreal 1,100-pound (499-kg) bite. It might be stronger; when I measured it, the squid ate my bite-force meter!

SAWFISH

MEET THE BEAST

THE SAWFISH IS ONE OF THE RAREST AND MOST ENDANGERED FISH on the planet ... not to mention one of the freakiest fishes you'll ever find. This 1,000-pounder (454 kg) looks like a 20-foot (6.1-m)-long flattened fish, with what looks like a hedge trimmer attached to its nose. The long, flat rostrum, or saw, on the tip of its nose is lined with supersharp teeth. That's right; it has teeth **outside its mouth!**

MOUTH

1²3 BY THE NUMBERS

THE ROSTRUM HAS BETWEEN 24 AND 28 TEETH on each side, totaling 56 outside the mouth. Inside the mouth are about 300 tiny rounded grasping teeth.

DID YOU KNOW?

THE ROSTRUM'S SENSORY ORGANS can detect the heartbeat of prey buried in the sand in front of the sawfish.

BITE FORCE

UNKNOWN AT THIS TIME. No one has been crazy enough to get up close and measure it, with that deadly swinging saw on its nose!

TEETH

WHAT'S ON THE
MENU

You might think that, with a saw on its nose that's lined with needle-sharp teeth, a **SAWFISH** would eat anything and everything it wants. That's surprisingly not the case. The sawfish is a bottom dweller that roots around in the sand with its rostrum to dig up **small crabs** and other invertebrates. It also eats small schooling fish like **herring** or **mullet** that it stuns, slashes, or gores with its swinging rostrum.

BITE BUSINESS

The sawfish is the **"slicer and dicer"** of the predator world. Its long, flattened rostrum is lined with permanent sharp, slender teeth, making it one of the most dangerous noses on the planet. When a hungry sawfish locates a school of fish, it explodes with a burst of speed and swings its saw from side to side. It slashes, cuts, and stuns the prey, then gulps up the injured fish. It's not swinging blindly, either. The sawfish can use the rostrum with great accuracy to spear a fish, then shake it off its snout before sucking it into its mouth, all in one lightning-fast motion. It has small teeth inside the mouth that grip and crush, but the rostrum teeth do all the damage. **And the saw isn't just for killing;** it's the ultimate multitool. It's flexible and covered with sensory organs that transform the saw into an early alert system and antenna that can detect prey and predators alike.

BULL SHARK

MEET THE BEAST

WITH ITS POWERFUL MUSCLES and barrel chest, this wide-headed shark looks like a bull with fins. (That's how it got its name!) And just like an angry old bull in front of a red flag, it's considered to be **one of the most aggressive sharks.** It's not a large shark—its maximum length is around 11 feet (3.4 m)—but it makes up for size with its big attitude.

1²3 BY THE NUMBERS

BULL SHARKS HAVE AROUND 150 TEETH: around 50 first-row teeth, plus two fully formed backup rows. The largest measure about an inch (2.5 cm) long.

DID YOU KNOW?

BULL SHARKS HAVE BEEN FOUND hundreds of miles upriver from the sea. Remember that next time you take a swim in your local river!

MENU

BULL SHARKS are not picky eaters; they'll eat just about anything that crosses their path. Of course, they concentrate on aquatic prey. **Fish, squid, stingrays, and turtles** are among their favorite fare. But anything swimming on the surface—ducks, snakes, small mammals—is fair game, too. In some locations, other **sharks** are their main food source. And if you happen to be another bull shark, you better keep your eyes open: Bull sharks are known to be cannibals!

BITE BUSINESS

Bull sharks often use a **bump-and-bite** feeding strategy. They bump things with their nose to check them out before they bite. It's kind of like how you might poke at your dinner plate before diving in. The bump is the good news; the bad news is definitely the bite! The bull has a wider head than most other sharks. A wider head usually means more muscle, and more muscle usually means more jaw power. Bull sharks are **one of the strongest biters** on the planet, and they're armed with lots of teeth. The upper teeth are wide, triangular, and strongly serrated—fantastic for slicing. The triangular lower teeth have finer serrations and are good for penetrating. The bottom teeth hold the prey while the upper jaw moves out and down with extreme force, driving those slicers in to do their damage. In addition, bull sharks have some pretty dirty mouths. (After all, animals don't have their moms reminding them to brush their teeth!) Tests have shown that bull shark teeth contain lots of bad bacteria. If the prey is lucky enough to survive the initial bite, it has to deal with massive infection later.

BITE FORCE

THE BITE OF THE BULL SHARK has been measured at more than 900 pounds (408 kg). That's about the same weight as a telephone pole.

Family Portrait

SHARKS

WHEN YOU THINK OF SHARKS, YOU PROBABLY THINK OF TEETH! You most likely have an image of a razor-sharp triangular-shaped tooth, like what's found in a great white shark's deadly jaws. But there are lots of different types of sharks, with lots of different types of teeth. Their chompers can tell you a lot about the shark's lifestyle, where it lives, and what it eats.

Cookie-Cutter Shark

Its sharp ice-cream scoop of a mouth gouges out chunks of meat from large prey like whales. They've even been known to take bites out of submarines!

Ragged Tooth Shark

It swims with its mouth open, showing off its traplike set of long, sharp, recurved teeth used for stabbing fish.

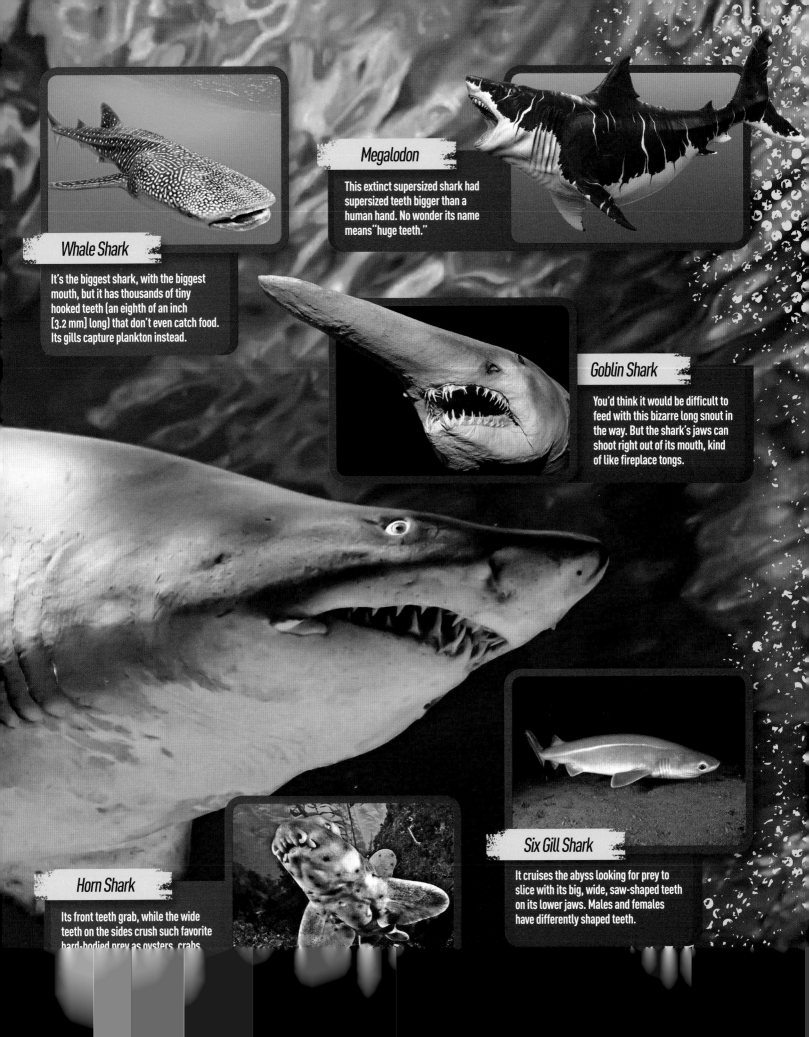

Megalodon

This extinct supersized shark had supersized teeth bigger than a human hand. No wonder its name means "huge teeth."

Whale Shark

It's the biggest shark, with the biggest mouth, but it has thousands of tiny hooked teeth (an eighth of an inch [3.2 mm] long) that don't even catch food. Its gills capture plankton instead.

Goblin Shark

You'd think it would be difficult to feed with this bizarre long snout in the way. But the shark's jaws can shoot right out of its mouth, kind of like fireplace tongs.

Six Gill Shark

It cruises the abyss looking for prey to slice with its big, wide, saw-shaped teeth on its lower jaws. Males and females have differently shaped teeth.

Horn Shark

Its front teeth grab, while the wide teeth on the sides crush such favorite hard-bodied prey as oysters, crabs

CHAPTER 3

CRUSHERS

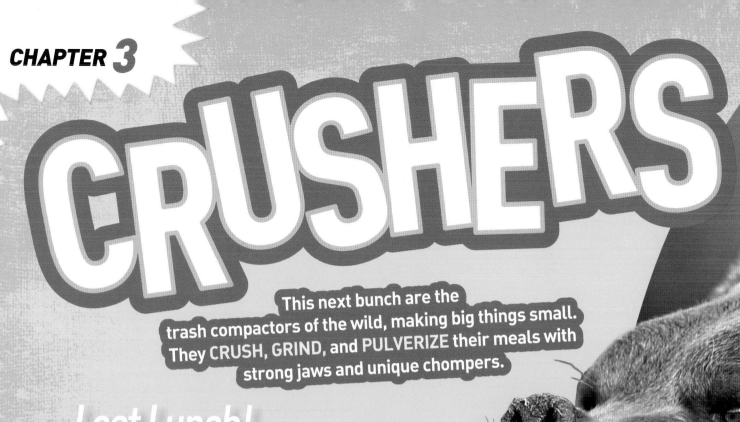

This next bunch are the trash compactors of the wild, making big things small. They CRUSH, GRIND, and PULVERIZE their meals with strong jaws and unique chompers.

Lost Lunch!

A FEW YEARS AGO I was studying grizzly bears and hoping to get some bite-force readings. I had National Geographic build a protective steel cage—for me, not the bear! The plan was for me to stay inside the cage and have a bear bite my pressure gauge safely outside the cage.

We traveled to Alaska to a place where bears were known to hang out. I climbed into my cage and waited for a bear to arrive. Boy, did I wait ... and wait, and wait! I sat in the cage for hours and nothing showed up. Around midday, I was getting super hungry, so I broke out my fried chicken lunch.

Before I could even take a bite, a bear lumbered out of the woods and right up to my cage. He didn't just come to my cage and sniff. He rocked the cage back and forth, then he pushed it over. He rolled my cage around, doing everything he could to get inside. **Yikes! I was sideways, upside down, then back right-side up.** I felt like a dog's chew toy being rolled around!

It was happening so fast I couldn't locate my bite-force meter. Things were flying around inside the cage and I was getting dizzy. It felt like I was in a washing machine and that I might vomit. I didn't know how much longer I could take it.

Suddenly, the bear stopped. What had happened? I thought maybe the door on the cage had come unlocked; I was scared. Then I noticed that my fried chicken leg had fallen outside the cage. The bear snatched it up and waddled back into the woods. **It was over just as quickly as it had started.** I was disappointed that I didn't get the bite-force reading, and I was also hungry because the bear had stolen my fried chicken. At least I wasn't on the bear's lunch menu!

On this expedition I found myself up a tree with nowhere else to go and a hungry bear trying to climb up and join me! It's a good thing fat bears aren't good climbers!

GRIZZLY BEAR

MEET THE BEAST

THIS IS ONE HUGE BEAST. It can stand more than 10 feet (3 m) tall on two legs, and on all fours it measures almost 5 feet (1.5 m) tall. It tips the scales at more than 1,000 pounds (454 kg), but it's no out-of-shape, overweight slowpoke. Grizzlies can run about as **fast as a racehorse,** so don't think you'll outrun one! They have grizzled brown fur and are characterized by a large hump on their back.

DID YOU KNOW?

IT'S ESTIMATED A GRIZZLY CAN EAT 40,000 moths in a day. That's like eating two moths every 14 seconds all day. Are there bathroom breaks?

BITE FORCE

SCIENTISTS HAVE USED computers to estimate the grizzly's bite force to be more than 600 pounds (272 kg). That's plenty to crush 40,000 moths!

MENU

When you're a big burly bear, you have a big burly appetite! **GRIZZLIES** need to eat around 20,000 calories a day. That's the calorie equivalent of eating more than 80 candy bars! (Talk about a sugar rush!) These big, ferocious bears might look like carnivores, but they're omnivores. They often eat mostly **plants**. They love **berries**, **seeds**, **grasses**, **sedges**, and **roots**. They also eat a lot of small insects like **grubs**, **moths**, **ants**, and **bees**. Small **rodents** and **fish**, especially **salmon**, are on the menu, too. Grizzlies are fish-catching specialists—no rod and reel needed!

BITE BUSINESS

Underneath the grizzly's hump and inside its massive head are big, strong muscles and a heavy skull, both indicators of a seriously large bite. The grizz can be defined as a brute, because it's a heavyweight crusher. (That sounds like a wrestler!) It doesn't need a specialized killing technique to bring down prey, like the jaguar and lion do. Grizzlies normally go after smaller prey like rodents, birds, squirrels, and other small mammals by overpowering them with their brute force. When you **weigh half a ton** (.45 t), you get to make a lot of the rules. So they also take down large prey such as deer, elk, and moose. They don't kill with a deadly bite, like the big cats, because they don't have the teeth for it. Grizzlies lack carnassials, those cutting blade teeth that the big cats are so proud of. **Their teeth are designed to grind, crunch, and crush.** They're powered by strong muscles attached to a massive skull. A grizzly's big canines and beefed-up incisors are great for holding onto prey, especially a slippery salmon or a struggling vole. The broad, flat molars in the back of the mouth crush prey and grind nuts.

1²3 BY THE NUMBERS

THEY HAVE 42 TEETH, with four impressive canines, the longest being around two inches (5 cm) long! That's the length of a house key.

AFRICAN ELEPHANT

MEET THE BEAST

YOU MAY HAVE USED THE PHRASE "BIG AS A HOUSE" to describe something large. Well, these creatures are the definition of big! African elephants are the planet's largest land animals. The biggest one ever recorded weighed 24,000 pounds (10,886 kg) and was 13 feet (4 m) tall! **That really is as big as a house!** With their long, flexible trunk, wrinkled skin, giant flapping ears, and ivory tusks, elephants are truly like nothing else.

1²3 BY THE NUMBERS

ELEPHANTS HAVE THE PLANET'S LARGEST TEETH. Tusks have been recorded at more than nine feet (2.7 m) and around 200 pounds (91 kg). They have 26 other teeth, too.

DID YOU KNOW?

IN THE SAME WAY THAT HUMANS are right- or left-handed, elephants are usually right- or left-tusked, using one tusk more than the other.

BITE BUSINESS

Meet the moving sidewalk of the animal tooth world. In most animals, replacement teeth move in from below or behind existing teeth. An elephant's new teeth move forward from the back of the mouth like a conveyor belt, with old teeth falling out of the front of the mouth. The massive molars are about the **size of a brick and can weigh five pounds** (2.3 kg). They're used to grind up vegetation. Unlike cows, goats, or horses—which chew in a side-to-side motion—an elephant grinds food forward and backward. Remember, elephants eat a lot, so essentially inside the mouth is nothing but molars and premolars. Elephants don't have canine teeth. But, boy oh boy, do they have upper incisors! You may know them as tusks. They are ginormous teeth (longer than you are tall) that **grow continuously throughout the life of the elephant,** at a rate of about seven inches (17.8 cm) a year. Like your baby teeth, elephants get two sets (baby and adult versions) of these massive pearly whites. The tusks are the elephant's multitool, used for digging, scraping, ripping, plowing, and, of course, as weapons.

WHAT'S ON THE
MENU

What do they eat? A lot! They're elephants! **AFRICAN ELEPHANTS** eat over 300 pounds (136 kg) of food a day, and it's all plants. Their staples are lots of **grasses, leaves,** and **fruits.** They love **tree bark,** too, which they strip off trees with their trunk and tusks. They also eat—prepare yourself, this is gross—their own **poop!** This practice is called coprophagia. They frequently eat their own poop because their digestive system isn't very good at absorbing all the nutrients from their food. So they re-eat it and send it back through a second time. Wow!

POOP

BITE FORCE

ITS BITE FORCE is unknown at this time. Elephants keep eating the bite-force meters!

REINDEER

MEET THE BEAST

HOOF

REINDEER ARE ALSO CALLED CARIBOU.
With their massive antlers, they look like really big deer—naturally, because they're members of the deer family. But unlike deer (where only males have antlers), both male and female caribou sport antlers. Reindeer stand about five feet (1.5 m) tall at the shoulder. They can weigh over 700 pounds (318 kg)—about the weight of two refrigerators! Their wide hooves act like snowshoes to support all that weight.

BITE FORCE

WE DON'T KNOW A REINDEER'S BITE FORCE, but it doesn't have to be strong to grind lichens. Maybe we can ask Santa to find out!

1 2 3 BY THE NUMBERS

REINDEER HAVE 34 TEETH—two more than a human—but they lack upper incisors. A big reindeer tooth is about the size of a postage stamp.

BITE BUSINESS

Meet the re-chewers! Reindeer belong to a group of animals called ruminants. These animals have specialized stomachs that use microorganisms to help break down plants, which are hard to digest. The word "ruminant" literally means "to chew over again," and that is what reindeer do. Like cows, goats, and giraffes, they chew their food awhile, then swallow it and let the microorganisms work on it. They then regurgitate, or vomit it back up, and chew on it a little more! Then swallow, vomit, chew, and repeat, repeat, repeat! Re-chewing effectively breaks down those tough plant fibers.

As you might suspect, reindeer teeth aren't designed for piercing and tearing, but are modified for some serious chewing. The premolars and molars are wide and flat and used for grinding. The incisors up front snip off grasses. But hold on for this: **They only have incisors on the lower jaw!** That's right—no incisors up top, no front teeth! Instead, they have a tough pad on the roof of their mouth that's kind of like the bottom of your foot. The lower incisors press against that pad to tear off grasses. That helps start the grinding process.

DID YOU KNOW?

A HUNGRY REINDEER can smell lichens under two feet (0.6 m) of snow!

LICHENS

WHAT'S ON THE MENU

REINDEER live in the far northern tundra, a type of ecosystem where the ground is always frozen and trees do not grow. It's a tough place to live if you're a plant-eater. During the winter, there's usually only one choice on the reindeer's menu: **lichens**. Lichens kind of look like plants but aren't. They are a combination of an **algae** and **fungus** living together. If you don't think that sounds tasty, you're not alone. Very few animals eat lichens. Fortunately, during the warmer summer months when more things grow, reindeer can find **grasses** and small **shrubs** to eat, too.

OUR LIMITED DATA SHOWS the bite force is around 30 pounds (13.6 kg), but it could be even stronger.

GILA MONSTER

MEET THE BEAST

MEET THE MONSTER! The Gila monster's fearsome reputation comes from its enormous, bulldog-like bite. It's the **largest lizard in the United States,** measuring one to two feet (0.3 to 0.6 m) long. Its bright skin—orange and black or pink and black—looks beaded because of bony interior plates that provide protection. Throw in a big fat tail, forked tongue like a snake, venomous bite, and beady eyes, and you have yourself a monster!

1 2 3 BY THE NUMBERS

MONSTERS HAVE around 40 sharp, recurved, replaceable teeth. They all look similar and are about a quarter inch (6.4 mm) long.

WHAT'S ON THE
MENU

Even though **MONSTERS** have a powerful, venomous bite, they don't need to use it for their favorite meal: **eggs**. Bird eggs, snake eggs, lizard eggs—they're all easy to break open and require little work on the monster's part. Gila monsters also eat invertebrates like **insects** and **spiders** and prey upon small **rodents, reptiles,** and **birds** as well. They even have been known to feed on **dead animals,** too. Gila monsters don't need to eat often. But when they do, they really chow down. Monsters can consume meals that weigh a third of their own body weight!

DID YOU KNOW?

GILA MONSTERS EAT ONLY THREE OR FOUR TIMES A YEAR. If you had only three meals a year, what would they be? I know what I'd pick: cake, cake, and more cake.

BITE BUSINESS

After a monster bites its victim, it hangs on tight and lets its **venom drip into the wound.** Locking on gives the venom a chance to get inside and work its magic. The monster has big solid lower teeth that have grooves along their length. The grooves **act as a pathway** for the venom to flow from the venom glands, along the lower jaw, and into the bite. The venom continues to flow as the Gila monster bites and chews on its victim. Strong adductor muscles—attached to an oversize skull—power the bite and drive the long, recurved teeth into the prey. Most of the time, though, a monster's prey is so small—like a mouse—that no venom is needed. The monster just grabs a rodent in its jaws and crushes its skull. Gila monsters don't chew their food; their teeth are **designed just for holding.** So they simply swallow things whole, just like a snake does.

RODENT

Human kids start losing their teeth around age six.

HUMAN

MEET THE BEAST

WOW, THIS IS A TOUGH ONE, because we are strange beasts to describe. Humans come in all shapes, sizes, and colors. How would you describe a human? We stand upright on two legs. We have two arms. A big, round head, housing our amazing brain, sits on top of our neck. We have grasping hands with opposable thumbs, to help us get around our environment. Like some other mammals, we live in **family groups,** and we eat lots of kinds of food!

BITE FORCE

A STRONG ADULT BITE is around 200 pounds (91 kg) of force. That's about the same weight as an entire adult male, teeth to toes!

CHILDREN HAVE 20 primary, or baby, teeth. Adults have 32 teeth. The largest teeth are about the size of your thumbnail.

BITE BUSINESS

Your teeth and jaw are pretty good at doing a lot of different things: cutting, snipping, cracking, gripping, and grinding. We have matching teeth on top and bottom, which come together when the mouth is closed. Adults have **32 permanent teeth,** divided in four different types. Starting up front and moving backward, you'll find incisors, canines, premolars, and finally the molars. The incisors snip and cut, like when you bite an apple. **The canines are good for gripping,** like when you're biting onto a turkey leg and trying to rip away some meat. The eight premolars smash the food you're chewing, like grinding up granola at breakfast. Kids don't have premolars because they come in with the permanent teeth, like the molars. Most adults have 12 molars. These are the grinders that really smash and break down food. Some people never **grow in all their molars,** especially the last ones in the back of the mouth. Sometimes, there just isn't enough room to accommodate any more teeth, so those stay tucked inside the gums. When that happens, they may have to be surgically removed. Yikes, that's not a lot of fun for anybody!

WHAT'S ON THE
MENU

We may not have as unique a set of teeth as other animals, but we do have especially hard teeth. They're the toughest things in **HUMAN BODY.** That's because we have superthick enamel (the protective outer layer of a tooth). Having hard teeth and a strong jaw allows us to eat pretty much anything, from **ice cream to hard foods like walnuts.** And though we have the teeth to crack nutshells, we usually don't. We're smart enough to know that using a nutcracker is much easier on our chompers. It's important to take care of our teeth, because unlike sharks, we only get one permanent set!

DID YOU KNOW?

THE RECORD FOR MOST TEETH in a human mouth is 37—that's 5 more than average. Order some extra toothbrushes!

BROWN RAT

MEET THE BEAST

THE BROWN RAT, also called the Norway rat, is a large rodent about 20 inches (51 cm) long (including its tail) that can weigh two pounds (0.9 kg). Its body is covered in thick brown fur. (Maybe that's why it's called the brown rat!) Its ears and tail are bald, and its tail is always shorter than its body. It has a **narrow pointed face with long yellow teeth.**

1 2 3 BY THE NUMBERS

RATS HAVE 16 TEETH, but only incisors and molars. The long yellow incisors up front are the longest, about a quarter inch (6.4 mm) long.

DID YOU KNOW?

IF A RAT DOESN'T CONSTANTLY WEAR DOWN its fast-growing incisors, they will pierce the roof of the mouth and brain, killing the rat. Talk about a headache!

BITE BUSINESS

With a strong bite, **rats are crushers.** But they're even better gnawers. To be a good gnawer, you need powerful muscles plus strong, sharp incisors, which rats surely have. The enamel on rat teeth is harder than iron, allowing them to gnaw through most anything. A rat's unique incisors grow constantly. They grow so fast that an incisor is never more than two months old! Rats must wear them down by gnawing or grinding them together. The incisors are harder on the front surface than they are on the back, so the teeth wear down faster in back. That gives them a chisel-like sharpness. The muscles that drive the incisors are really powerful because they are attached far forward on the skull. One of them even goes through the eye socket, which causes the rat's eyes to vibrate back and forth when it's gnawing hard. It would be almost impossible for a rat to read while having a snack! **The muscles are also fast-acting, allowing the rat to bite six times a second.** See if you can do that! Rats don't have canine teeth, but they do have 12 grinding molars in the back.

WHAT'S ON THE
MENU

RATS are successful because they're opportunistic omnivores, meaning they eat almost anything. A rat restaurant menu would run several pages long. Some highlights include **fruits, nuts, vegetables, plants, leaves, grains, fungi, insects, birds, eggs, amphibians, reptiles,** and other **small mammals.** They also practice coprophagia (eating their own poop). That sounds gross, but it helps them utilize nutrients that weren't absorbed during the first pass through the rat! Whenever rats come across more than they can eat, they cache it. That means to hide it somewhere to eat later. Have you ever cached that last piece of apple pie? Be honest!

BITE FORCE

RATS CAN BITE with almost 30 pounds (13.6 kg) of force. That's enough to gnaw through cement or even a lead pipe!

HYACINTH MACAW

MEET THE BEAST

THIS IS ONE BIG, BEAUTIFUL BIRD. In fact, it's the largest parrot on Earth. It measures about three feet (0.9 m) long with a five-foot (1.5-m) wingspan. This giant of the parrot world **lives only in South America.** Though big, it's light. It weighs around three pounds (1.4 kg)—less than one of your textbooks. It gets its name "hyacinth" from its brilliant bluish purple coloration, like the flowers of the same name. A bright yellow ring circles each eye, and a sharp beak completes the picture.

BITE FORCE

ITS BITE FORCE HAS BEEN MEASURED at almost 170 pounds (77 kg). That's nearly 60 times the macaw's body weight!

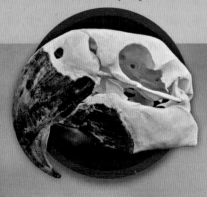

DID YOU KNOW?

A HYACINTH MACAW CAN CRACK OPEN a coconut with its powerful beak! Man, that's not just crazy strong but coco loco strong!

MENU

A macaw's diet might drive you nuts, because that's what they eat: nuts, nuts, and more nuts. The MACAW could be nicknamed the nutcracker, because that's what it's all about, cracking nuts! They crack big nuts, little nuts, soft nuts, but especially hard nuts. Because other birds can't open them to eat them, there's more for the macaws to chow down on. In fact, you'd need a hammer or heavy nutcracker to open such macaw favorites as Brazil nuts and palm nuts. Sometimes macaws like a little salad with their nuts. They also dine on certain plants, flowers, fruits, and leaves.

BITE BUSINESS

The thickness of its beak determines a bird species' jaw strength and diet. A macaw has a wide, thick beak, which is more powerful than a narrow beak. It is covered in a hard protein called keratin, the same substance in your fingernails and hair. The keratin reinforces those bills so they can crack nut after nut. The bill also has a bite-force secret. The macaw doesn't swing open only its lower bill, like you do when you drop open your bottom jaw. The macaw's upper bill has a hinge that allows it to swing open, too. This gives the macaw a wider gape and more force in biting. But that's not all! The macaw's tongue is a lot different than yours. It's dry and scaly, and it has bones inside of it. (It's actually more like your finger than your tongue.) The macaw uses its tongue to manipulate a nut just right, so that the seam of the nut is positioned along the cracking edge of the lower mandible. The tongue finds the perfect place along the bill to crack different-size nuts. The tongue then separates the cracked nut's hard shell from the tasty seeds inside!

1 2 3 BY THE NUMBERS

YOU'LL FIND NO TEETH HERE, just a powerful, strongly hooked beak made of keratin, the same stuff that your hair is made out of.

HIPPO

MEET THE BEAST

DO YOU THINK OF HIPPOS AS CUTE, CHUBBY ANIMALS? Don't be fooled: They're one of the largest, most dangerous animals on the planet! Big ones can weigh three tons (2.7 t), which places them right behind elephants in size. Despite their round body and stubby legs, hippos can **run surprisingly fast,** about 30 miles an hour (48 km/h). That's as fast as a car on a city street. They have a surly attitude and some of the animal kingdom's largest teeth.

1²3 BY THE NUMBERS

A HIPPO NEEDS A JUMBO-SIZE MOUTH—about four feet (1.2 m) across—to house its 40 massive canines and incisors.

DID YOU KNOW?

A HIPPO CAN OPEN ITS MOUTH about 180 degrees. That's straight up and down! You can only open your mouth about 40 degrees.

HIPPOS are herbivores, so they're all about the salad bar. They spend most of their day in the water. When their stomach starts growling in the afternoon, it's time to feed. They venture out of the water and eat **savanna grasses** throughout the night. Their diet is almost 100 percent grass. It takes a lot of grass to satisfy a hungry, hungry hippo. They eat around 150 pounds (68 kg) of grass a night. They're very protective of their favorite feeding areas, so they mark them with their poop! Please don't try that around your kitchen refrigerator!

BITE BUSINESS

Hippos have one of nature's most **impressive sets of chompers.** Its mouth is more than four feet (1.2 m) wide, one of the biggest and strongest in the animal kingdom. Its humongous mouth is armed with giant curved canine teeth that measure almost two feet (0.6 m) long—about the length of your arm—and are constantly growing. Its long, straight incisors can reach one foot (0.3 m)! So why such big, honking teeth, you ask? Not for feeding, that's for sure! They use them to stab and wound other hippos in territorial battles. Hippos sometimes display their impressive front teeth with a wide-open yawn to **scare off rivals,** like you flexing your muscles at a bully. It's the teeth in the back of the mouth that do all the work of eating. Hippos specialize in **eating grass**—lots of it. Their big rubbery lips rip up vegetation and move it toward the massive, flat molars in the back, which are the pulverizing and grinding machines. Since hippos eat only grass, their molars are vitally important. When the molars get too worn down to be effective, the hippo needs to start making funeral arrangements, because it's end of story!

BITE FORCE

ITS BITE FORCE IS MORE THAN 1,800 (816 kg). That's almost a ton (0.9 t), the weight of a small car!

Brady's BITE Story

HIPPOPOTAMUS

Hello, Hippo Lips!

ONE OF THE CLOSEST CALLS I EVER HAD WAS WITH A HIPPO. I was working on a project to measure the bite force of a hippo. It's the second largest land animal on the planet, yet amazingly its bite force has never been measured. I was curious as to why it had never been tested before, but confident I could get it.

Measuring bite force is pretty easy. All you have to do is get the animal to bite down on a bite-force meter. The plan was for me and my crew to enter a zoo's hippo enclosure and **get close enough for the hippo to bite down on the meter without biting down on me.** I had the meter attached to an extralong pole so I wouldn't have to get too close.

As we entered the hippo's enclosure, I could see that the zookeeper had drained the hippo's pool of water so that it would be easier for us to work. That made the hippo really mad! As I inched closer, the big hippo opened her massive mouth, and I got a personal view of those giant tusks. Yikes! She shook her head and seemed really bothered that we were in her enclosure. As I held my breath, I extended the long pole toward her gaping maw.

Suddenly, the two-ton (1.8-t) animal charged! I was frozen with fear. Somehow my brain got my legs to start working, and I turned and ran. It was chaos: People were screaming, the hippo was bellowing, kids were crying, and I was running for my life with that angry hippo right on my tail!

As I headed for the only gate in the enclosure, I saw that there was a traffic jam of people all trying to get out, too. As my crew fought each other to get through the small door, I frantically swerved to the left and headed for the fence. It was not a second too soon: The massive hippo was almost on top of me! **I stumbled a few more steps before launching myself into the air,** attempting to jump the fence. As I did, I felt the big, rubbery, slime-covered hippo lips on the back of my leg! Double yikes!

The fence was really tall, more than five feet (1.5 m), something that I could never jump over in a million years. But I had no choice. I was about to become lunch for this hungry, hungry hippo!

Somehow, some way, the miracle of all miracles occurred. I actually made it over the fence and to safety on the other side. Boy, was that hippo mad! She shook her head and bellowed at me. I was dazed and confused, bruised and battered. **I just had a hippo's lips touch my leg?** Good grief! I shook with the thought and instantly understood why the bite force of the hippo had never been measured before. It's just way too dangerous!

Top: Male hippos will use their massive gape and giant tusks to challenge each other. You definitely wouldn't want to get in there to break up the squabble!

Right: One of the most dangerous animals on the planet is a protective mother hippo that's with her baby. Even the fiercest crocodiles know to give her space—lots and lots of it!

FERAL HOG

MEET THE BEAST

FERAL HOGS LIVE ON THE WILD SIDE! Their ancestors were once domestic animals, like farm animals. They even look somewhat like farm pigs. But once these hogs went feral, or wild, their appearance changed. Feral hogs **grow tusks.** Their back hair is thick and bristly. They can get huge—up to 1,000 pounds (454 kg)! And boy, can these humongous hogs get aggressive! They **travel in groups called sounders** and can be dangerous to humans.

1 2 3 BY THE NUMBERS

FERAL HOGS HAVE 44 TEETH. Their constantly growing tusks, or canines, can measure more than eight inches (20 cm) long. That's longer than a pencil!

DID YOU KNOW?

WHEN PIGS ARE BORN, they have needlelike teeth that stick out of their gums sideways. Yikes! That sounds more like a cactus than a pig!

MENU

Have you heard the phrase "eat like a pig"? Well, **FERAL HOGS** do eat like pigs—probably because they are pigs! They're opportunistic feeders, meaning that they take every opportunity to devour anything and everything that they come across. These omnivores love **berries, nuts, bird eggs, plants, roots, snails, insects, spiders, reptiles, amphibians,** and **small mammals.** They've even been known to prey on baby deer! They are especially good at rooting around in the ground with their tusks for **worms, fungi,** or tasty **roots.** They can destroy crops in the process, which makes them a huge problem for farmers.

BITE FORCE

ITS BIG-TIME BITE FORCE MEASURES over 400 pounds (181 kg), equal to a wolf's. The wolf might want to think twice about blowing down this pig's house!

BITE BUSINESS

Male feral hogs are called boars; females are called sows. They both have two upper tusks and two lower tusks, but boars have larger tusks than sows. The tusks are **oversize canine teeth that constantly grow.** The lower ones curve backward out of the mouth in a semicircle shape, and they can be super sharp. These lower canines or tusks are called cutters, because hogs use them to **slice and cut.** The upper tusks are called whetters. They are named after a device, called a whetstone, that's used to sharpen a knife. That is exactly what the whetters do: They sharpen the cutters. The cutters constantly grind against the whetters, and that friction keeps them razor sharp. The lower tusks are used for slashing and stabbing and can be serious weapons, making a feral hog one dangerous animal to come across. The tusks are also good for **digging food,** such as tasty onions or potatoes, out of the ground. The grub is quickly crushed and ground in the back of the mouth by the numerous molars and premolars. They have a total of **28 grinding teeth,** which could make the feral hog the poster child of the crushers!

CHAPTER 4

GULPeRS

These BIG MOUTH critters have BIG APPETITES and love big meals, so they tackle their hunger by using BIG GULPS! They use their unique feeding methods and large mouths to master the art of gulping.

Shocking Experience

I WAS ON A TRIP TO VENEZUELA and on the lookout for my favorite turtle, the mata mata. I had never seen it in the wild, so I was eager for an opportunity to get my hands on one and do some bite research! I found a local guide who took me to a small stream. He said I would have a good chance of finding a mata mata there.

I figured that the best way to catch a mata mata would be to drag a long net across the bottom of the stream. **I crossed my fingers, waded into the water,** threw my net out, and started pulling. The net soon felt heavy and started moving in my hands. **I definitely had something—a lot of something!**

I dragged my net into the shallows for a closer look. I had captured lots of stuff: loads of fish, some eels, some turtles. Among the wiggling fish, I spied what I was after. It was my prize: **a mata mata!** I quickly reached into the water to grab my turtle.

WHAM! Like a bolt of lightning, I was zapped off my feet. I felt stunned, dazed, and in pain! I was in such agony that I almost bit off my tongue! I staggered out of the water. **I felt like my teeth had just melted,** my hair was on fire, and I had smoke coming out of my ears. My guide yelled, "ELECTRIC EEL!" Yikes! I had just been zapped with **600 volts of "Hello!"** and lived to tell about it!

I got a memorable two-for-one that day. I had seen my first mata mata and also experienced my first electric eel! I did get a bite-force reading that day, but it wasn't from the turtle. It was from me biting down on my own tongue!

AN UNEXPECTED FIND

1²3 BY THE NUMBERS

LIKE ALL TURTLES, mata mata has zero teeth, but instead uses its big, flexible mouth to grasp prey when needed.

MATA MATA TURTLE

MEET THE BEAST

YOU SAY "WHATA WHATA?" I say "mata mata!" This is one of the strangest-looking animals around. It wrote the book on camouflage: It looks like a pile of leaves. The mata mata is a **South American turtle** with a long neck and a snorkel for a nose. It has an undersized shell and a big triangular head. It's sometimes called the smiling turtle, because head on, it looks like it has a **smile** on its face!

DID YOU KNOW?

THE NAME MATA MATA COMES FROM a Spanish word meaning "kill." Perhaps a small fish created that name, because they're the mata mata's main victims.

BITE BUSINESS

The mata mata isn't really a biter. It's more of a **gulper**—and definitely a strange-looking character. These reptiles are super-suction feeders. When a tasty fish gets close enough for an attack, the mata mata sucks it up in the blink of an eye. It is a fantastic way to get food, and it all starts with the neck. Its long neck shoots out toward the meal, like a spring-loaded snake jumping out of a can. It happens fast—really fast! A feeding strike and recoil occurs in less than **20 milliseconds** (two-hundredths of a second), about the time it takes for a hummingbird to flap its wings once. As it shoots its head toward a fish, the turtle simultaneously opens its mouth wide and uses muscles to rapidly expand its throat and mouth area, which creates suction. The mata mata instantly gets a mouthful of water and fish. It then squeezes the water out between its clenched lips, leaving a fish meal behind in the mouth. The turtle **swallows its prey whole** and is ready to launch the next super-sneak attack on unsuspecting prey!

SNOUT

BITE FORCE

ITS BITE FORCE IS LESS than a pound (0.5 kg), but that's no problem. What matters instead for the mata mata is speed and suction.

••••• WHAT'S ON THE •••••

MENU

The **MATA MATA** is one good fisherman. You have to be if you eat practically nothing but fish! It's a sit-and-wait predator, so like all good anglers, the mata mata has a lot of patience. Its long neck and face are covered with small fleshy projections and barbels, filament-like sensory organs that help detect prey. These also break up the turtle's outline and hide it from potential prey. Plus, small fish may view these fleshy bits as something to eat, so they swim in for a closer look. That is their last mistake, because the mata mata quickly gulps them up.

AMERICAN BULLFROG

MEET THE BEAST

THIS IS ONE BIG FROG! The American bullfrog is the **largest frog** in North America, at eight inches (20 cm) long and weighing more than a pound (0.5 kg). The largest ones can be about as big as a **baseball cap.** Right behind its big brown eyes are very large tympani, or external eardrums. Long, powerful rear legs give the bullfrog fierce jumping skills. It's a spotted green jumping machine!

MENU

The **PYTHON'S** menu features warm-blooded prey, big and small. They eat all sorts of mammals, like **rats, rabbits, antelope, monkeys, bats,** and even **porcupines. Birds** are warm-blooded, so they make the hit list, too. Pythons have heat-sensitive organs lining their lips, enabling them to track down warm-blooded prey. They can even hunt in total darkness, which means **bats** in a cave are fair game, too. They're also capable of eating gigantic meals three times bigger than themselves. That would be like you sitting down and eating a 200- to 300-pound (91- to 136-kg) cheeseburger—that you have to swallow whole!

BITE BUSINESS

Drop anchor! That's what the African rock python might say right before it bites, because it uses its bite solely as an **anchoring point.** The snake's teeth hold on to prey until its body's powerful squeezing coils can take over. Pythons are **constrictors,** which means that they squeeze their prey to death. African rock pythons have over 10,000 muscles—about 15 times the number in your body! The python's muscles generate a tremendous force that prevents blood from flowing around a victim's body and kills it. Inside the mouth is a scary-looking set of needlelike teeth. The python has lots of teeth, including two rows of large teeth on the roof of its mouth! It's teeth city in there! The replaceable teeth are recurved, ensuring that whatever goes in doesn't get back out. The teeth also help in directing food down the hatch. Snakes don't chew their food, and they don't have hands to help out, so they **swallow everything whole.** They work their flexible jaws and skull around their meal—which is sometimes much larger than their own head—and maneuver until it is gulped down.

DID **YOU** KNOW?

PYTHONS CAN GO MORE THAN A YEAR without feeding. Imagine leaving the breakfast table one morning and saying, "See you in a year, Mom!"

Family Portrait

SNAKES

LOVE THEM OR HATE THEM, snakes are one of the most successful groups of animals on Earth. They're found just about everywhere, on every continent except Antarctica. You might think that they all look and act alike. But with more than 3,000 different types of snakes, there are big differences in the snake family, especially in the way they CHOMP!

Cottonmouth

The young have bright yellow tail tips, which they wiggle to lure in fish and other prey.

Inland Taipan

This Australian snake is considered by most experts as having the deadliest bite on the planet, because it has the most toxic venom.

Spitting Cobra

Its hollow fangs have openings on the front, not the tip. This allows it to spit venom.

Yellow Anaconda

These big South American snakes eat crocodiles and caimans. But if they're not careful, their meal eats them!

Emerald Tree Boa

This beauty has long narrow, extrasharp teeth that it uses to penetrate a bird's feathers to eat one of its favorite meals.

King Cobra

The longest venomous snake on the planet is called "king" for good reason. It eats other snakes—lots of them—by grabbing them with its powerful jaws and then slurping them down!

Gaboon Viper

This venomous African snake's two-inch (5-cm) fangs are the longest of any snake. It has to fold these stabbers up to fit them inside its mouth!

Eastern Hognose

When a toad inflates its body to keep from being swallowed, an eastern hognose uses its oversize rear fangs to pop it like a balloon!

Clouded Snake

This is one fine diner. It enjoys eating escargot—snails! It uses its long teeth on the lower jaw to pop snails out of their shells.

Egg-Eating Snake

Invite this serpent over for brunch! It's the ultimate egg lover, using vertebrae on the roof of its throat to crack open the shells.

CRAB-EATING SEAL

MEET THE BEAST

CRAB-EATING SEALS ARE THE PLANET'S most abundant seal. You can find these seals hanging out in **family groups** on pack ice in the Antarctic. They're big seals, weighing close to 400 pounds (182 kg) and measuring around seven feet (2.1 m) long. If you get a good look at their long bodies, it's not unusual to see scars. Those come from their sworn enemies, the leopard seals, that try to eat them!

BITE BUSINESS

Talk about a misleading name. This beast should be called the krill-eating seal, because that is about the only thing it eats. It has incredibly **unique teeth** that it uses to capture its minuscule prey. Its molars are multilobed, with fantastic curly projections coming off of the sides. They look like a work of art and unlike any teeth you have ever seen. The seal doesn't use them for cutting, grinding, snipping, shearing, or slicing. They only have one function: **straining.** Here is how they work. Crab-eaters mainly feed at night because that is when krill move into somewhat shallower water. The seal will take a deep dive to locate a large group of krill, then swim through them with its mouth open. The mouth fills with both water and krill. The seal then shuts its mouth and forcefully expels the water through its tightly clenched intricate teeth, leaving just the krill behind in the mouth. The interlocking teeth act just like a **pasta strainer,** separating krill from water. The mouthful of krill is then gulped down whole.

YUM!

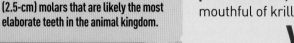

1 2 3 BY THE NUMBERS

THEY HAVE 34 TEETH, including one-inch (2.5-cm) molars that are likely the most elaborate teeth in the animal kingdom.

DID (YOU) KNOW?

THE SCIENTIFIC NAME OF THE CRAB-EATING SEAL, *Lobodon,* comes from a Greek word meaning "lobed teeth." And boy, are they ever!

KRILL

BITE FORCE

ITS BITE FORCE IS UNKNOWN.
These seals are about filtering, not biting. Besides, nobody has volunteered to brave an Antarctic ice floe for a measurement.

•••••••• WHAT'S ON THE ••••••••

MENU

What does the menu say? "All-you-can-eat krill!" **Krill** make up more than 90 percent of the **CRAB-EATING SEAL**'s diet. Krill are tiny crustaceans that look like shrimps. They're found in deep cold waters of the Antarctic. They're small—only around two inches (5 cm). However, they're the most abundant animals on Earth, so there's a lot of them out there. They hang out together in massive groups called clouds, which makes chowing down on them pretty easy. Oh yeah, they're also bioluminescent (they give off light), so they're easy to find as well.

EASTERN DIAMONDBACK RATTLESNAKE

MEET *THE BEAST*

IT DOESN'T TAKE A GENIUS to recognize this guy. It has a rattle on the end of its tail, and a diamond-shaped pattern on its back. It's the **largest rattlesnake** in the world, growing to around eight feet (2.4 m). It has a big triangular head, an unblinking stare (snakes don't have eyelids), and a lightning-fast venomous bite. So watch out! Lucky for us, its rattle **warns of its presence** before it strikes. Thanks, rattler, we owe you one!

DID YOU KNOW?

THE RATTLESNAKE CAN STRIKE FASTER than human reaction time. If you're in the strike zone—about one-third of the snake's body length—there's no escape!

90

BITE FORCE

ITS BITE FORCE IS UNKNOWN, BUT LIKELY WEAK. Instead of a strong skull for biting, a rattlesnake has a flexible skull for swallowing giant meals.

BITE BUSINESS

Rattlesnakes have lots of small teeth that are used for gripping prey. The exceptions are its big fangs. These serpents are **wonders of nature**. The fangs are long and hollow, like hypodermic needles. They inject venom deep into prey. They're so long that they have to be **folded against the roof of the mouth** when they're not in use. They're kept safe in a soft-tissue sheath, just like you might keep a sword in a scabbard. When they are in use, watch out, because rattlesnakes have one of the fastest bites on Earth. When a strike begins, the jaws open nearly **180 degrees,** and the head flings forward faster than you can blink your eyes (around one-fifth of a second). The folded fangs suddenly swing open and into position. They're quickly driven into the prey to deliver the venom. When the bite is over, the snake recoils just as quickly as it struck. The fast-acting venom not only kills the prey, but it also starts digesting it from the inside out. The snake then gulps it down whole.

····• WHAT'S ON THE •····
MENU

Warm-blooded prey are the special of the day—every day—on the rattlesnake's menu. **RATTLESNAKES** are pit vipers. They have specialized organs (pits) on the front of their face that allow them to detect temperature differences. They don't see like you do. Instead, they see things as a thermal image (different levels of warm and cold). This allows them to hunt warm-blooded prey, like **mammals**, in complete darkness. Known favorites include **rats, mice, squirrels, rabbits,** and **birds.** Rattlesnakes can eat larger animals—prey bigger than the size of their mouth—because they have superflexible jaws and skulls.

123 BY THE NUMBERS

RATTLERS HAVE AROUND 100 **REPLACEABLE TEETH.** Their deadly fangs measure more than one inch (2.5 cm) long.

After Bite

CONGRATULATIONS! YOU'VE CHOMPED YOUR WAY THROUGH THE BOOK! (ARE YOU FULL YET?) These animals have opened wide and shown you how their **BITES ARE MUCH, MUCH MORE THAN JUST THE WAY THEY EAT.** An animal's body structure and design provide us invaluable clues to how they thrive and survive. The more we learn about animals today—especially ones that are endangered or threatened with extinction—the better we can **PROTECT** them and ensure their **SURVIVAL.**

However, it's not enough to protect just the animal. We also need to protect the things that are **IMPORTANT TO THAT ANIMAL:** its breeding grounds, nesting habitat, water, and of course, food! For example, it doesn't do the very endangered Chinese alligator much good if it is protected but its habitat is ruined, food sources are destroyed, or other resources vital for the animal's existence are **WIPED OUT.**

It's not always easy to figure out what is important for a particular animal. You see, some animals are extremely rare and seldom, if ever, seen. Some are not only shy but also well camouflaged. Some live in harsh environments or places that are difficult or dangerous for researchers to go, like the

deep ocean. Some animals are simply really dangerous to work with. So basic information, such as what an animal eats, can actually be very difficult to determine.

That's why scientists have to **DIG FOR CLUES.** Researchers study an animal's teeth, the shape of the jaw, its muscles and skull. These all provide clues about an animal's feeding habits and food sources. But more than that, they **TEACH** us how much power it packs behind its bite to kill prey and defend itself.

Scientists use that same approach to learn about animals of the past, too. We all know that extinction means gone forever. One of the best and only ways that researchers can learn about extinct animals like the dodo bird, woolly mammoth, and *T. rex* is to study their fossils for clues about what was important to them when they were still alive. And maybe, just maybe, those hints from the past may help us better understand and protect other animals that are alive today.

NOW YOU'RE PART OF THE BITE TEAM, TOO! The next time you come across an animal skeleton, tooth, jaw bone, or skull—whether in a museum or out in nature—examine it closely. (If it's labeled, don't peek!) Use what you have learned from this book and see if you can find the clues that unravel the mystery of the **CHOMP!**

Further Resources & Glossary

FURTHER RESOURCES

Brady Barr with Kathleen Weidner Zoehfeld. *Crocodile Encounters!* National Geographic Kids Books, 2012.

Brady Barr with Kathleen Weidner Zoehfeld. *Scrapes With Snakes!* National Geographic Kids Books, 2015.

Lucy Spelman. *National Geographic Animal Encyclopedia.* National Geographic Kids Books, 2012.

SuperCroc. National Geographic Videos, 2002.

GLOSSARY

apex predator A predator at the top of the food chain that no other animal preys upon

canine One of a mammal's four pointed teeth

barbel A filament-like sensory organ that helps certain aquatic animals detect prey

incisors Sharp teeth at the front of a mammal's mouth

maxillary teeth Teeth in the upper jaw

molars Large teeth at the back of a mammal's mouth, used for crushing or grinding

protrusible When part of the body can be extended or thrust forward

ruminant A mammal that brings up food from its multichambered stomach and chews it again

serrated Having a row of sharp points

vomerine teeth Teeth on the roof of a frog's mouth

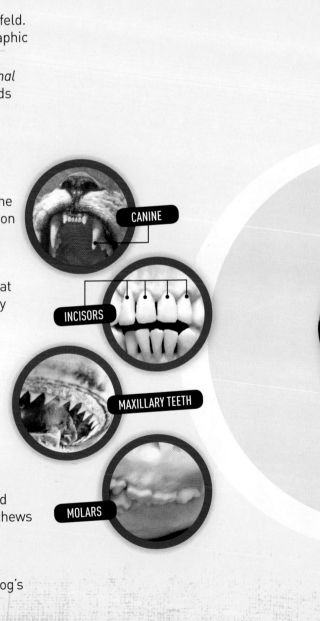

CANINE

INCISORS

MAXILLARY TEETH

MOLARS

Acknowledgments & Credits

DEDICATION AND ACKNOWLEDGMENTS

I would like to dedicate this book to my mom and dad. They have always supported my love of animals and our natural world. They were there for my very first bite, by a monkey at the local zoo when I was three years old. I also would like to acknowledge the scientists and researchers all over the world whom I've had the privilege of working alongside while studying some of the most amazing animals on Earth. The animals and researchers have taught me so much. In addition, a special shout-out to my National Geographic Television field crews. They've witnessed so many bites firsthand and were instrumental in keeping me safe and well taken care of in some of the most remote and dangerous places on the planet. Lastly, thanks go out to all the wild animals I have been so fortunate to interact with during my career, and for them not removing any of my body parts during those interactions. For that I am truly grateful. —BB

The author and publisher wish to thank the book team: Kristin Baird Rattini, Shelby Alinsky, Kathryn Williams, Sarah J. Mock, Eva Absher-Schantz, Julide Dengel, Alix Inchausti, and Anne LeongSon.

Text Copyright © 2017 Brady Barr

Compilation Copyright © 2017 National Geographic Partners, LLC.

Published by National Geographic Partners, LLC. All rights reserved. Reproduction of the whole or any part of the contents without written permission from the publisher is prohibited.

Since 1888, the National Geographic Society has funded more than 12,000 research, exploration, and preservation projects around the world. The Society receives funds from National Geographic Partners, LLC, funded in part by your purchase. A portion of the proceeds from this book supports this vital work. To learn more, visit natgeo.com/info.

NATIONAL GEOGRAPHIC and Yellow Border Design are trademarks of the National Geographic Society, used under license.

For more information, visit nationalgeographic.com, call 1-800-647-5463, or write to the following address:

National Geographic Partners
1145 17th Street N.W.
Washington, D.C. 20036-4688 U.S.A.

Visit us online at nationalgeographic.com/books

For librarians and teachers: ngchildrensbooks.org

More for kids from National Geographic: kids.nationalgeographic.com

For information about special discounts for bulk purchases, please contact National Geographic Books Special Sales: specialsales@natgeo.com

For rights or permissions inquiries, please contact National Geographic Books Subsidiary Rights: bookrights@natgeo.com

Art directed by Eva Absher-Schantz and Julide Dengel

Designed by James Hiscott, Jr.

Trade paperback ISBN: 978-1-4263-2839-8
Reinforced library binding ISBN: 978-1-4263-2840-4

Printed in Hong Kong
17/THK/2

ILLUSTRATION CREDITS

Credit Abbreviations: SS = Shutterstock; GI = Getty Images; MP = Minden Pictures; ASP = Alamy Stock Photo; NGC = National Geographic Creative

FRONT COVER: (lion), Andrew Lam/SS; (shark), Tim Davis/Corbis/VCG/GI; (hippo), Richard Du Toit/MP; (snake), Kevin Horan/GI; SPINE: Ignacio Yufera/MP; BACK COVER: (crocodile), Bill Birtwhistle/GI; (shark), Tim Davis/Corbis/VCG/GI; (lion), Tom Brakefield/GI; (bear), Paul Souders/GI; (squid), Reinhard Dirscherl/GI; (snake), Joel Sartore/NGC; (Brady), Brad Talbott; INTERIOR: 1, Theo Allofs/MP; 2-3, David Fleetham/ASP; 4 (UP), dive-hive/SS; (LO), zhengzaishuru/SS; 5 (ALL), Courtesy Brady Barr; 7, Mitsuaki Iwago/MP; (UP LE), EastVillage Images/SS; (UP RT), Cindysaz1/Dreamstime; (dot texture all), Hudiemm/GI; 8, Anup Shah/MP; (LO), Bone Clones; 9, Moizhusein/SS; (UP), Sean Crane/MP; (LO), jaroslava V/SS; (cardboard all), Tolga Tezcan/GI; 10-11, Krystyna Szulecka/ASP; 10 (UP), Dave Watts/MP; (LO), Bone Clones; 11 (CTR), Bildagentur Zoonar GmbH/SS; (LO), Susan Flashman/SS; 12, Holly Kuchera/SS; 13, Steve Ard/Tracker Aviation Inc/NGC; (UP), Stayer/SS; (LO), Bone Clones; 14-15, Naluphoto/Dreamstime; 14 (UP), Mico Siren/ASP; (LO LE), dive-hive/SS; 15 (CTR RT), Ryan M. Bolton/SS; (LO LE), Skulls Unlimited; 16-17, Michael and Patricia Fogden/MP; 16 (LO), Anup Shah/NPL/MP; 17 (UP LE), Biju Boro/AFP/GI; (CTR RT), Jiang Hongyan/SS; (LO LE), Skulls Unlimited; 18 (UP LE), Brad Talbott, Courtesy Brady Barr; 19 (ALL), Courtesy Brady Barr; 20, Michael and Patricia Fogden/MP; (CTR), Patrick Fagot/MP; 21, Steve Winter/NGC; (UP), Skulls Unlimited; (CTR), Aneese/GI; 22-23, David Havel/SS; 22 (CTR LE), Ana del Castillo/SS; (CTR RT), Kritsada Promyim/SS; (LO), Mari Swanepoel/SS; 23 (UP), Bone Clones; 24-25, Pete Oxford/MP; 24 (UP), Stephan Bonneau/MP; 25 (UP LE), Matyas Rehak/Dreamstime.com; (UP RT), Sui Lun Lee/GI; (CTR), Lukas Blazek/Dreamstime; (LO RT), Michael Rosskothen/SS; (LO CTR), Gallo Images/GI; 26-27, Boris Diaw; 26 (LE), Suzi Eszterhas/MP; 27 (UP), Skull Unlimited; 28-29, Herschel Hoffmeyer/SS; 28, Marques/SS; 29, Herschel Hoffmeyer/SS; 30-31, Bart Breet/MP; 30 (LE), Robert Preston Photography/ASP; (RT), Chris and Tilde Stuart/MP; 31 (UP), Bone Clones; 32-33, Kurt G/SS; 32 (CTR), Mark Moffett/MP; (LO), Bazzano Photography/ASP; 33 (UP LE), Nature Picture Library/ASP; (UP RT), Eric Isselee/SS; (CTR), irin-k/SS; 34, Courtesy Brady Barr; 35, Boaz Yunior Wibowo/Dreamstime.com; 36-37, Daniel Heuclin/MP; 36 (LO), Tischenko Irina/SS; 37 (LO), Bone Clones; 38-39, Courtesy Brady Barr; 39 (LO LE), Ryan M. Bolton/SS; (RT), Eric Isselee/SS; 40-41, ilbusca/GI; 40 (UP), Sylvain Cordier/Biosphoto; (LO RT), Vadim Petrakov/SS; (LO LE), guentermanaus/SS; 42-43, Richard Susanto/SS; 42 (UP), dbimages/ASP; (CTR), Patrick Rolands/SS; (LO), Bone Clones; 43, Sergey Uryadnikov/SS; 44 (UP LE), Brad Talbott; (CTR), Courtesy Brady Barr; 45 (UP), Courtesy Brady Barr; (CTR), WaterFrame/ASP; (LO), Mauricio Handler/NGC; 46-47, Carrie Vonderhaar/Ocean Futures Society/GI; 46 (LE), Franco Banfi/MP; (RT), Courtesy Brady Barr; 47 (LE), David Wrobel/SeaPics; (RT), Bob Cranston/SeaPics.com; 48-49, Charline Tetiyevsky/Dreamstime; 48 (CTR), Stephen Kajiura/SeaPics.com; (LO), Nature Picture Library/ASP; 49 (RT), Visual and Written SL/ASP; 50-51, Alexander Safonov/GI; 50, Norbert Wu/MP; 51 (UP), Jens Kuhfs/GI; (LO), Skulls Unlimited; 52-53, Atthapol Saita/SS; 52 (UP RT), Norbert Wu/MP; 53 (UP LE), Krzysztof Odziomek/Dreamstime.com; (UP RT), Herschel Hoffmeyer; (CTR), Kelvin Aitken/VWPics/ASP; (LO RT), Greg Amptman/SS; (LO LE), Douglas Klug/GI; 54, Courtesy Brady Barr; 55, Dennis Donohue/Dreamstime; (UP, LO), Courtesy Brady Barr; 56-57, Thomas Mangelsen/MP; 56 (CTR), Donald M. Jones/MP; (LO), Skulls Unlimited; 57 (CTR), ppl/SS; (LO), Breck P. Kent/NGC; 58-59, Anup Shah/GI; 58 (LO), Steve O. Taylor (GHF)/MP; 59 (LE), Skulls Unlimited; (RT), Anke van Wyk/SS; 60-61, Frans Lanting Studio/ASP; 60 (UP), Gordon Wiltsie/NGC; (LO), Dan Kosmayer/SS; 61 (UP), Skulls Unlimited; (LO), Bildagentur Zoonar GmbH/SS; 62, Michael D. Kern/MP; (UP LE), Skulls Unlimited; 63, Donald M. Jones/MP; (UP), Rick & Nora Bowers/ASP; (CTR), chuyuss/SS; (LO), Eric Isselee/SS; 64-65, Image Source Plus/ASP; 64 (LO), Bone Clones; 65 (LE), Carol Yepes/GI; (RT), Nataliia Pyzhova/SS; 66-67, Erni/SS; 66 (LE), Nigel Cattlin/ASP; (RT), Andrew Darrington/ASP; 67 (LE), Skulls Unlimited; (RT), Cube/GI; 68-69, Pete Oxford/MP; 68 (LO), Skulls Unlimited; 69 (LO), Pete Oxford/MP; 70, Giovanni De Caro/Dreamstime; (RT), Gerry Ellis/MP; 71, Mariusz Prusaczyk/ASP; (LE), Bone Clones; (RT), Christophe Courteau/MP; 72 (UP LE), Brad Talbott; (RT), Courtesy Brady Barr; 73 (UP), Thomas Finkenst_dt/EyeEm/GI; (LE), Courtesy Brady Barr; (RT), Tom Brakefield/GI; 74-74, Naturfoto-Online/ASP; 75 (UP LE), Jausa/SS; (UP RT), jps/SS; (CTR), Irina Ukrainets/Dreamstime; (LO LE), Skulls Unlimited; 76, Courtesy Brady Barr; 77, Michael and Patricia Fogden/NGC; 78-79, Nick Gordon/NPL/MP; 78 (UP), D and L Klein/Science Source; 78 (LO), Courtesy Brady Barr; 79 (UP), Jason Edwards/NGC; (RT), Kletr/SS; (LO CTR), Skulls Unlimited; 80, Kenneth H. Thomas/Science Source; 81, Treat Davidson/MP; (LE), Philip Dowell/GI; (RT), PeJo/SS; 82-83, Amanda Nicholls/SS; 82 (UP), frantisekhojdysz/SS; 83 (UP LE), Yann Hubert/SS; (UP RT), Alex Mustard/MP; (CTR), zhengzaishuru/SS; (LO LE), Courtesy Brady Barr; 84-85, Courtesy Brady Barr; 84 (UP), Bone Clones; (LO), Courtesy Brady Barr; 85 (UP CTR), Jabruson/MP; 86-87, JoeFotoSS/SS; 86 (UP), Jo Crebbin/SS; (CTR), NHPA/SuperStock; (LO), Stuart G Porter/SS; 87 (UP LE), ChameleonsEye/SS; (UP RT), Isselee/Dreamstime; (UP CTR RT), Frank Schneidermeyer/GI; (LO CTR RT), Kurt_G/SS; (LO RT), Mike Raabe / Design Pics/GI; (CTR LE), Danita Delimont/GI; 88-89, Doug Allan/MP; 88 (UP), Steven J. Kazlowski/ASP; (LO), Dmytro Pylypenko/SS; 89 (UP), Dmytro Pylypenko/SS; (CTR), I. Noyan Yilmaz/SS; (LO), Vicki Beaver/ASP; 90-91, Pete Oxford/Minden Pictures/GI; 90 (CTR), Pete Oxford/Minden Pictures/GI; (LO LE), Danita Delimont/GI; 91 (CTR LE), Skulls Unlimited; (CTR), Tyrone Turner/GI; 92 (LE), BGSmith/SS; (UP RT), Jiang Hongyan/SS; 93 (canine), Martin Withers/MP; (incisors), Bone Clones; (maxillary), Cultura RM/ASP; (molars), Bone Clones; (RT), jaroslava V/SS; 95 (RT), Nataliia Pyzhova/S; 96, Ignacio Yufera/MP

Index